MW01097557

Introduction to Bookbinding & Custom Cases

A Project Approach for Learning Traditional Methods

Tom Hollander | Cindy Hollander

SCHIFFER
PUBLISHING

4880 Lower Valley Road · Atglen, PA 19310

Other Schiffer Books by the Authors:

Constructing and Covering Boxes: A Beginner's Guide, ISBN 978-0-7643-3158-9

Other Schiffer Books on Related Subjects:

Prints Galore: The Art and Craft of Printmaking, with 41 Projects to Get You Started, Angie Franke, ISBN 978-0-7643-5628-5

Fountain Pens and Pencils: The Golden Age of Writing Instruments, George Fischler & Stuart Schneider, ISBN 978-0-7643-2839-8

Upcycling Books: Decorative Objects, Julia Rubio, ISBN 978-0-7643-5875-3

Copyright © 2019 by Tom Hollander and Cindy Hollander

Library of Congress Control Number: 2018958794

All rights reserved. No part of this work may be reproduced or used in any form or by any means—graphic, electronic, or mechanical, including photocopying or information storage and retrieval systems—without written permission from the publisher.

The scanning, uploading, and distribution of this book or any part thereof via the Internet or any other means without the permission of the publisher is illegal and punishable by law. Please purchase only authorized editions and do not participate in or encourage the electronic piracy of copyrighted materials.

"Schiffer," "Schiffer Publishing, Ltd.," and the pen and inkwell logo are registered trademarks of Schiffer Publishing, Ltd.

Designed by Molly Shields
Cover design by Brenda McCallum
Type set in Archer/Times New Roman

The endpapers, a rare hand-marbled butterfly pattern, were designed by and are courtesy of Galen Berry.

ISBN: 978-0-7643-5735-0
Printed in Serbia
5 4 3 2

Published by Schiffer Publishing, Ltd.
4880 Lower Valley Road
Atglen, PA 19310
Phone: (610) 593-1777; Fax: (610) 593-2002
E-mail: Info@schifferbooks.com
Web: www.schifferbooks.com

For our complete selection of fine books on this and related subjects, please visit our website at www.schifferbooks.com. You may also write for a free catalog.

Schiffer Publishing's titles are available at special discounts for bulk purchases for sales promotions or premiums. Special editions, including personalized covers, corporate imprints, and excerpts, can be created in large quantities for special needs. For more information, contact the publisher.

We are always looking for people to write books on new and related subjects. If you have an idea for a book, please contact us at proposals@schifferbooks.com.

Pamphlet book.
5½" × 8½" × ⅛"

To our two children, Jessica and Daniel, and three

grandchildren, Oliver, Chloe, and Allegra

To Cindy's parents, Bud and Cleola Long

To Tom's parents, William and Annette Hollander

Flat-back book with slipcase.
Book 5½" × 7" × ¾", slipcase
5¾" × 7¼" × 1"

CONTENTS

As with many activities in people's lives, book and box making appeared in Tom's life unexpectedly. Tom's mother, Annette Hollander, a highly accomplished artist, took a bookbinding class and developed her own simplified process of making books, boxes, and other creative items. She used traditional bookbinding tools and techniques but streamlined the steps to make the process as simple as possible. These skills allowed her to start a small cottage industry called Bookcraft in Hamden, Connecticut in the 1970s.

When Tom was fourteen, his mother began teaching him these techniques. He helped her for many years making books, boxes, and a variety of unique desk accessories. In 1986 Tom and his wife, Cindy, set out to build a similar business in Ann Arbor, Michigan. Tom and Cindy continued much of what his mother had developed, and at the outset they made hundreds of hand-crafted books and boxes that they sold at art and craft shows throughout the Midwest. In 1991, they opened a small retail store selling their handmade products. They soon expanded their business and began selling decorative papers and bookbinding supplies, as well as offering workshops as Hollander's School of Book and Paper Arts.

Over the years, Tom and Cindy continued to refine their book and box making skills and in 2009 they wrote their first book—*Constructing and Covering Boxes: A Beginner's Guide*. In their new book, *Introduction to Bookbinding & Custom Cases*, Tom and Cindy share the skills they have been practicing and teaching for many years. With its focus on making five individual projects, their new book offers a unique approach for learning a centuries-old traditional craft form. Enjoy limitless possibilities as you hone your skills and create your own unique books and boxes.

Round-back book with clamshell box.
Book 5½" × 6" × 1", clamshell box 6" × 6½" × 1¼"
Flat-back book with slipcase.
Book 5½" × 7" × ¾", slipcase 5¾" × 7¼" × 1"

ACKNOWLEDGMENTS

We would like to thank Maureen Hollander for her expertise in reviewing and editing our book. From traditional book-binders Eric Alstrom, Jon Buller, Don Etherington, and Monique Lallier, we appreciate their valuable comments, suggestions, and long-time support. Thank you to Judith Lowe, who read our earliest drafts and offered guidance in getting us started with this book. We wish to express our most sincere gratitude to our friends Joe and Karen O'Neal. Their continued confidence in our abilities made it possible for us to have a successful and rewarding business for over twenty-five years in the Kerrytown Market & Shops in Ann Arbor, Michigan. Finally, thank you to Pete Schiffer, Sandra Korinchak, and the staff at Schiffer Publishing for believing in us and working with us to write this book.

Round-back book with clamshell box.
Book 5½" × 6" × 1", clamshell box 6" × 6½" × 1¼"

INTRODUCTION

Introduction to Bookbinding & Custom Cases is a step-by-step guide for learning beginning- and intermediate-level skills for bookbinding and box making. There are five projects in this book, including three for making books and two for making cases or boxes to hold books. Each project begins with a recommended list of materials, tools, and supplies, along with project dimensions. Detailed instructions with many images ensure success in completing the project. The first two chapters of the book lay the foundation for getting started in bookbinding and box making, while chapters 3 through 7 are the individual projects. Before beginning the projects, we recommend reading through each for a general overview.

A collection of books, boxes, and tools

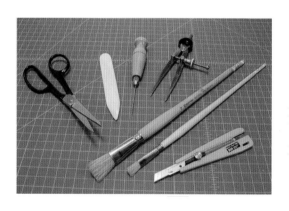

Chapter 1, "Basic Materials, Tools, and Supplies," introduces the items we recommend for use with the projects. Most of these are fairly inexpensive and easy to acquire, and no major equipment is necessary for completing the projects. Some of the items are optional and the projects could be completed without them. A number of reliable sources are listed in the back of the book to help you find your tools and materials.

A few basic tools recommended for the projects

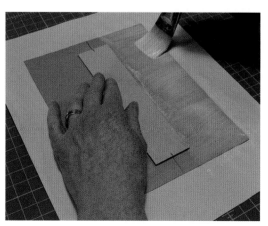

Chapter 2, "Fundamentals and Methods," includes several broad prerequisites that are useful for completing the projects. These include understanding and determining grain direction and learning various methods for measuring and cutting. In addition, we discuss adhesives, gluing techniques, and tips. Throughout the project chapters, we offer more-specific methods that are common to traditional bookbinding and box making. These include learning several sewing styles, casing-in a text block, and construction and covering techniques that are specific to slipcases and boxes.

Adhesives and gluing methods are discussed in **chapter 2.**

Chapter 3, "The Pamphlet Book," is the first project. This type of book is a great introduction to traditional bookbinding in its simplest form, with a focus on learning a very basic sewing technique. The pamphlet book style is popular for printing your own short works, then binding the text pages and the cover together as a single signature. Because the soft cover pamphlet book does not require any gluing, it is an easy structure for beginners. We chose to use a standard 8½" × 11" text paper, making it easy to format and print yourself.

The pamphlet book is a great starter book.

Chapter 4, "The Flat-Back Book," is a traditional hard cover book structure. As the name implies, this book incorporates a flat, narrow spine. With this project you will learn the process of sewing multiple signatures, tipping in flyleaves, attaching spine reinforcement, gluing endpapers, adding headbands, and casing-in the text block. The flat-back is a structure suited for thinner books with approximately three to six signatures and is usually under 100 pages. This project uses a slightly smaller page size than the Pamphlet Book project.

The flat-back book utilizes many components found in traditional bookbinding.

Chapter 5, "The Round-Back Book," includes many of the same components as the flat-back but emphasizes a more sophisticated spine structure. A rounded spine can accommodate a greater number of signatures, and the hollow tube attached to the spine enables the book to open and close easily. The book includes a trim strip, adding a decorative element to its covers. For this project, we designed a thicker book of 12 signatures and 200 pages, starting with 5 ½" × 10" text paper. With its rounded spine and concave fore-edge, this compact structure has a pleasing aesthetic quality.

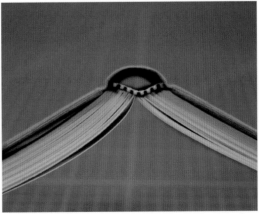

The round-back book features a hollow-back spine and is designed to accommodate many more pages than the flat-back book.

Chapter 6, "The Slipcase," is essentially a box or case with one open end. This elegant structure provides basic protection for a book or set of books. One of the challenges in constructing the slipcase is getting the measurements accurate enough so that the slipcase is neither too tight nor too loose for the book. We offer measurement tips on how to make the slipcase just right. The project is specifically designed to store the flat-back book; however, it can be resized to hold any book, including the round-back.

The slipcase is designed to house the flat-back book.

Chapter 7, "The Clamshell Box," shows how to construct and cover one of the sturdiest box structures available for holding books. Sometimes referred to as a drop-spine box, it is composed of two trays and a lid that lies perfectly flat when opened. The drop spine allows for the book to be easily removed from its tray. Because this box offers the maximum amount of protection from sunlight and dust, it is a popular design for use with rare or one-of-a-kind books. The clamshell box project has been designed to house chapter 5's round-back book project, but its versatility enables it to also store valuable documents, photographs, and art prints.

The clamshell box is designed to hold the round-back book.

Chapter 8, "Book and Box Making Formulas," lists all the formulas needed for cutting your own flat-back and round-back books, slipcases, and clamshell boxes. We also include how to measure the dimensions of a book so that it will correspond to the measurements needed to construct slipcases and clamshell boxes. Examples of each formula in this chapter conveniently start with a standard-size text paper of 8½" × 11" for building the text block. This will enable you to simply follow the example measurements if you choose to use text paper of this size.

Customize your books and boxes with the measuring guidelines and formulas.

Chapter 9, "Gallery of Books and Boxes," includes various custom books and boxes we've made that can be used both for inspiration and as a reference. Most of the items have been constructed using traditional methods, although some non-traditional styles are included and may offer ideas for designing your own books and boxes.

The gallery showcases a variety of books and boxes we have made.

The appendix includes a table that converts fractions to millimeters and decimals, as well as a convenient chart that helps determine various paper weights as related to pounds and grams. This chart will make it easy to select your text paper for sewing signatures.

The glossary defines terms commonly used in bookbinding and box making. Most of these terms are used throughout the book; however, the glossary also contains additional terms you can expect to run across as you advance in bookbinding and box making. The chapters where you can find more information are listed after each description. The terms are also listed in the index.

To further advance your skills, the "Book and Box Making Resources" section contains useful books and workshop opportunities. Sources for bookbinding materials, tools, and supplies are also provided.

Hollander's School of Book & Paper Arts

Basic Materials, Tools, and Supplies

The projects in this book use readily available materials, tools, and supplies. Optional but recommended items are marked with an asterisk (*). When the term "traditional" bookbinding and box making is used, we are referring to the basic materials, tools, and techniques that have been used for the past century or longer. Sometimes, however, there is a more recent product or tool that has been adopted by traditionalists, such as PVA glue and Teflon folders.

BASIC MATERIALS

Beeswax*

Beeswax is commonly used in bookbinding to lightly coat linen sewing thread. It helps prevent thread from tangling and adds a small amount of tack to help hold the thread in place during the sewing process.

Beeswax is used to lightly coat your sewing thread.

Book Board

Book board is a primary material used in bookbinding and box making. There are various names used to describe book board, including binder's board, cover board, and chipboard. Davey board is a commercial name used to identify a denser and higher-grade book board. The thickness of book board varies and is generally measured in thousandths of an inch but listed in decimal format. Typically, book board thickness ranges from .060 (1/16") to .120 (1/8").

For all the projects in this book, we recommend a thickness of approximately .090 (3/32"). We have developed all the projects and formulas to accommodate this standard thickness. Using a board that is significantly thinner than .080 or thicker than .095 may require some minor adjustments to the formulas.

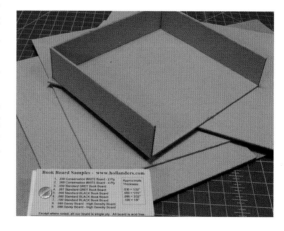

Book board ranges in thickness and density.

A common board thickness is .090 or 3/32".

Book Cloth

Book cloth is an exceptionally strong material that is commonly used for covering book board. When constructing books and boxes, book cloth is often used as the material for covering the spine because it is so much more resistant than paper to wear. It is not uncommon to cover an entire book or box in book cloth for durability.

Most book cloth is fabric that has been starched or coated in some manner to make it more durable. It comes in various textures, including a linen (coarse) or vellum (smooth) finish. Some book cloth is manufactured as an imitation leather, while some others have a paper backing which makes it easier to apply glue.

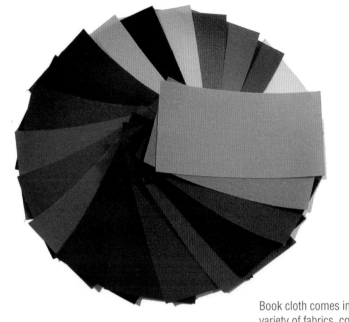

Book cloth comes in a variety of fabrics, colors, textures, and coatings.

Decorative Papers

There are countless options for using decorative papers as a covering material. Although some people prefer their books and boxes made in solid colors, it is more fun to choose from an assortment of hand-marbles, Florentine prints, Japanese silkscreens, or other exotic papers. We have been fortunate in our business to specialize in decorative papers and enjoy the wide array of patterns and styles of papers available to us from all over the world.

Regardless of what paper you choose, it is important to make sure that it is an appropriate thickness or weight for covering books and boxes. Generally, we suggest using a decorative paper with a text weight of about 70 lbs. (105 grams per square meter [gsm]). This equates to the weight of a good-quality copy paper. See "Text Paper" and the appendix for more information regarding paper weight.

Hand-marbled and printed papers from Brazil, India, Italy, Japan, and Thailand

Headbands*

Traditionally, headbands are sewn into the head and tail of the text block as a decorative support to the spine of a book. Most bookbinders today use commercial presewn headbands. Although we list headbands as optional, they are inexpensive and add such an attractive finishing touch to a handmade book that they are difficult to resist. Commercial headbands come in a variety of styles and colors and can often be purchased in small quantities from bookbinding suppliers.

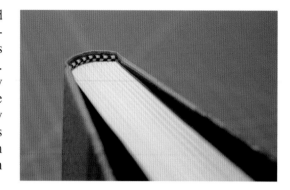

Decorative headbands add a finishing touch.

Kraft Paper

Kraft paper is a slightly coarse paper that is commonly used for making the hollow tube that attaches to the spine of the round-back book. Because of its durability, we also use kraft paper to wrap and protect the text block as we work on the spine. Kraft paper can be found in sheet form or on rolls. Kraft paper shopping bags can also be cut to the appropriate size and used if needed.

Kraft paper is used for the hollow tube in a round-back book.

Methyl Cellulose*

One of the most popular additives to PVA is methyl cellulose, which makes PVA easier to spread and helps extend the drying time. Methyl cellulose comes in powder form and easily mixes with warm water. We suggest a mixture of one to two tablespoons of powder to one pint of warm water. A more detailed description of its use can be found in chapter 2, "Fundamentals and Methods."

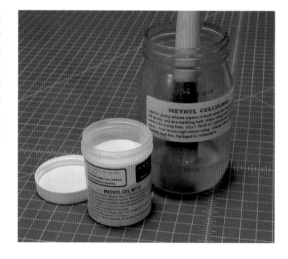

Methyl cellulose extends drying time of PVA.

PVA

There are many adhesives used in bookbinding. One of the most popular is a synthetic product called PVA (polyvinyl acetate). Bookbinding PVA is specifically formulated as an acid-free, non-yellowing, and permanently flexible adhesive. It is ideal for gluing the spines of books and boxes but can be used throughout the gluing process. PVA is relatively quick drying, which can be both a plus and a minus. The fact that it dries quickly means you will need to work a little faster, but it also means you can move through the steps quicker than when using a traditional vegetable glue such as wheat paste.

We use two different thicknesses of PVA. One is a thinner version that has a consistency like cream. We refer to this glue in our book as simply PVA. The other thickness is a much more concentrated version, which we call PVA-Thick. See chapter 2, "Fundamentals and Methods," for how to apply these glues and other types of adhesives.

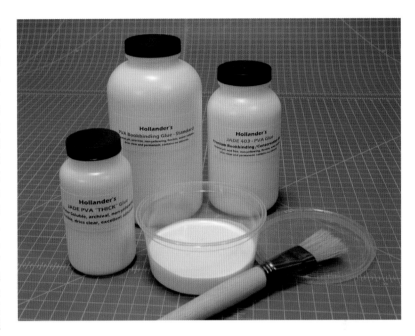

PVA is the most commonly used bookbinding adhesive.

Sewing Thread

Sewing thread used for bookbinding should be strong enough to be pulled taut while sewing and withstand repeated opening and closing of a book. Thread made from Irish linen is known for its strength and is the most widely used. A medium-thickness sewing thread is labeled 25/3, which we use for most of our book sewing. The "25" represents the thread's diameter, and the "3" represents the number of strands. An 18/3 thread would be thicker than 25/3, while one labeled 30/3 is a thinner thread.

Traditional bookbinding thread is unwaxed, but it is common to add a light coat of beeswax for stiffness and tack. Bookbinding thread can be purchased prewaxed, but the coating is often too thick for sewing signatures. Prewaxed thread, however, is popular for exposed sewing structures and is used in the pamphlet book project.

A variety of sewing threads for bookbinding

Super

One of the most common spine reinforcement materials used in bookbinding is called super. Super is a loosely woven cotton material that is heavily starched. It is attached directly to the spine by using PVA. Then it is glued to the insides of a book case and covered by the endpapers. It is the primary material for securing the text block to the case and is essential for making a strong book structure.

Super is a spine reinforcement material.

Text Paper

Text paper is the paper that is folded into signatures in the process of constructing a text block. Having a basic understanding of the weight of text paper either in pounds (lbs.) or grams per square meter (gsm) is a good starting point for selecting your paper. High-quality text paper has a "weight" range from 60 lbs. (90 gsm) to 80 lbs. (120 gsm). See the chart in the appendix for classifying and understanding the different weights of text paper.

Text paper is folded into signatures.

BASIC TOOLS

Awl

An awl is used for piercing holes into folded text pages prior to sewing. We suggest a thin awl, which produces a smaller hole than most traditional awls. Sometimes these awls are referred to as needle awls, paper awls, or bookbinder's awls. The purpose of the thinner awl is to produce a slightly larger hole than the needle itself. This helps keep the sewing thread as tight as possible in relation to the size of the hole that is being pierced. A makeshift awl may be fabricated by inserting the eye of a sewing needle into a cork.

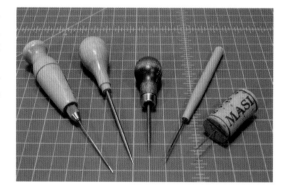

A variety of awls appropriate for bookbinding

Bone Folder

A bone folder is one of the most frequently used and indispensable tools used in bookbinding and box making. It has a multitude of uses, including folding and creasing text papers, rubbing down glued paper, and pressing material along the edges and into the corners of boxes. A 6" pointed bone folder is the most common size and style. Bone folders may be cleaned by washing them with soap and warm water.

Some folders, such as those made from Teflon, are synthetic and function very much like a genuine bone folder. Teflon folders allow you to rub the surface of the paper or book cloth without burnishing the material. However, a Teflon folder is not as effective in creating a crisp crease when folding text paper.

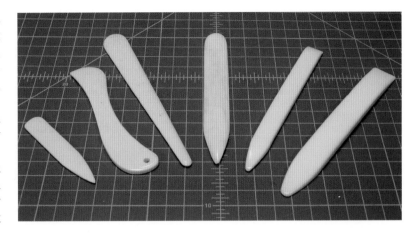

Folders in a variety of shapes, sizes, and materials

C-clamp

A C-clamp is used in the slipcase project and holds a support board to the workbench while you are building and squaring the side walls. A large spring clamp or other method to secure a support board to your workbench can be improvised.

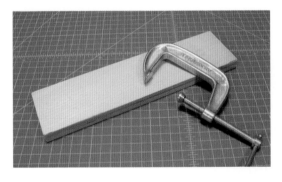

Use a C-clamp with support board when building a slipcase.

Cutting Knives

You will need both light-duty and heavy-duty knives for cutting your materials. Typically, lighter-weight cutting knives are used for cutting paper and book cloth. For cutting through book board, it is essential to use a heavier knife. Make sure to have plenty of spare blades or break-off refills and replace them frequently, especially when cutting thick book board.

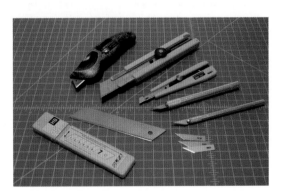

Light-duty and heavy-duty cutting knives with refills

Cutting Mat

A large cutting mat is an ideal surface for cutting book board and paper. A self-healing mat will help reduce dulling of the blades while cutting. To accommodate larger sheets of book board, paper, or book cloth, the larger the cutting mat the better. For the projects in this book, we recommend a cutting mat that is at least 18" × 24". It is also helpful if the cutting mat has a full set of ½" grid lines and ⅛" increments to assist you in measuring and cutting. See chapter 2 to learn the process for cutting your materials.

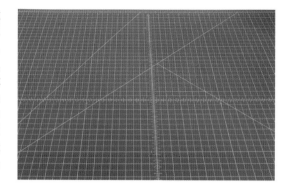

Cutting mat with grid lines

Glue Brushes

Almost any flat or round brush with natural bristles will work for gluing. A high-quality brush is a good investment and will last a long time, provided you thoroughly clean the brush with warm water. It is helpful to have several different sizes of brushes. A good starting point is to have at least two brushes, one that is a ½" in width and another that is 1". We prefer a flat brush over a round brush, but both are commonly used by bookbinders. In chapter 2 you will learn more about brushes and various gluing techniques and tips.

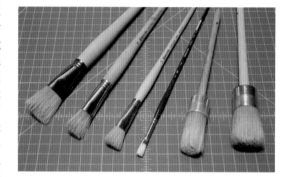

Good-quality natural-bristle brushes for gluing

Hammer

For round-back binding, a hammer is needed for rounding the spine. Almost any fairly heavy (10 to 16 ounce) hammer with a large and clean face, such as a household claw hammer, will work for this purpose. Although it is not essential, the best hammer for rounding a spine is one with a face that has a slightly convex shape, much like a cobbler's hammer.

A heavy hammer is used to round the spine of a book.

Makeshift Tools*

Using various makeshift tools such as measuring guides, weights, squares, and wire joint rods is common in bookbinding, and they are easy to fabricate. They are discussed in more detail in chapter 2, as well as in the appropriate project chapters.

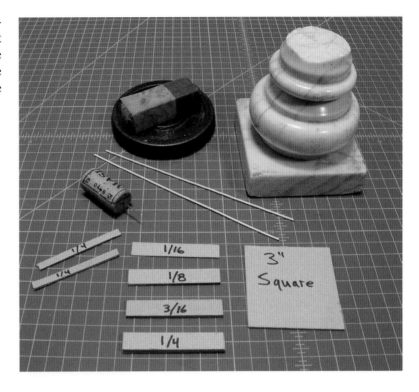

Common makeshift tools

Microspatula*

This inexpensive tool enables you to apply glue in hard-to-reach places. A microspatula may be used for touching up a small unglued area or adding glue to a spot that a brush might not be able to reach, such as in the corner of a box. It can also be used for lifting glued paper off the waste sheet, keeping your fingers free of glue. We use a light-duty knife in the same manner.

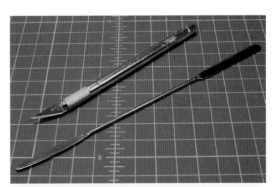

A microspatula or X-Acto knife helps apply glue in hard-to-reach places.

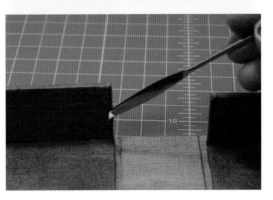

Press Boards*

We recommend using press boards before placing a weight on your finished books or boxes, instead of using a book press. The boards help disperse weight evenly across the surface of the structure. Placing a heavy weight or several heavy weights on top of the pressing board will ensure that your books and boxes dry flat and stay flat.

Press board is used when drying books and boxes.

Rulers and Cutting Bars

An assortment of rulers, straightedges, and heavy steel cutting bars are essential for measuring and cutting your paper, book cloth, and book board. Make sure your rulers are calibrated in $\frac{1}{16}$".

For cutting book board, we recommend a thick gauge, stainless-steel cutting bar. A heavy bar helps prevent slippage and keeps the book board stable on your mat. See chapter 2 for instructions on accurate cutting and measuring.

An assortment of rulers and cutting bars

Scissors and Shears

Because cutting and mitering is so much a part of bookbinding and box making, a high-quality pair of scissors or shears is an important and worthwhile investment. A medium-length (6" to 8") shears with a sharp point at the tips is ideal. Keep your scissors and shears clean of glue by washing the blades with soap and warm water and thoroughly drying. One of the best cutting tools we have found for bookbinding and box making is the Wiss bent-handle shears.

High-quality scissors are an indispensable tool.

Sewing Needles

It is important to use the right size of needle when sewing. Bookbinder's needles are stronger than most sewing needles; however, the needle chosen for a project must also be thin enough that it does not create a hole much larger than the thickness of the thread. When selecting a needle, consider the thickness of the thread and attempt to match the thread size with the eye of the needle. A #1 size eye will accommodate 18/3 thread; a #3 size eye, 25/3 thread; and a #5 size eye, 35/3 thread. If the size of the needle is not apparent, some trial and error may be required to get the proper size eye to match the thread diameter.

Eye of needles should match thickness of sewing thread.

Sponge*

We like to use a small sponge for dampening commercial papers before applying PVA. Dampening the paper on the side that will be glued allows the paper fibers to absorb moisture and stretch, making it easier to apply to book board. We will dampen almost all commercial decorative papers before applying glue, which helps prevent the paper from wrinkling. See chapter 2 for more information on using a sponge to "relax" papers.

Use a sponge to prestretch commercial papers.

Spring Divider*

A spring divider is a common measuring tool for bookbinders. A divider has two pointed ends and is a great alternative to using a ruler for making repeated measurements. Although we list this item as optional, we think you'll find it to be a worthwhile purchase for making quick and accurate measurements.

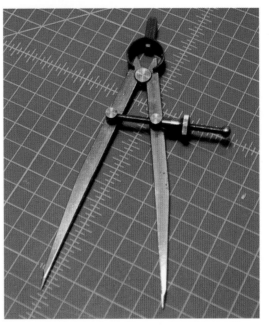

A spring divider is useful for repeated measurements.

Squares*

A large carpenter's square or L square is helpful for assuring that your book board is cut square. We also use a small steel square for measuring the dimensions of a book for a slipcase or clamshell box. A small steel square is heavy enough to use as a light weight.

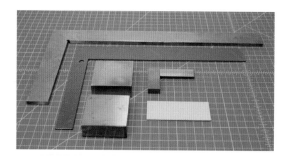

Squares are helpful for measuring accuracy.

Weights

Heavy weights are essential to ensure that your book board dries flat and stays flat. Makeshift weights work well, and almost anything that is relatively compact and heavy can be used. We have used covered bricks, heavy books, and even slabs of marble. Lighter weights are useful for holding text block signatures and other items in place while working with them.

Small and large makeshift weights

Wire (Joint) Rods

Thin wire joint rods are a useful item to include among your tools, especially when making case bindings. A couple of narrow wire rods (1/16") are ideal for forming a tight joint or groove along the hinge of a book. We discovered that wire clothes hangers are an appropriate thickness. Simply cut the long bottom piece from the hanger with a wire cutter. Knitting needles, specifically size 0, can also be used for this purpose.

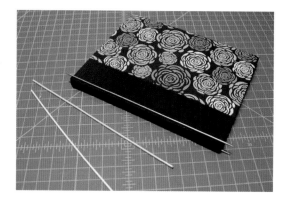

Thin wire rods are used to help define joints.

OTHER SUPPLIES

Damp Cloth

A damp cloth is handy to have nearby to help keep your fingers clean of glue. Be careful not to place the cloth where it can accidentally rest against your work and get it wet. It is best to keep it in an open plastic container.

Masking Tape

Masking tape can be used to temporarily hold together the uncovered sides of boxes that have been glued together, especially if they tend to warp. Painter's tape loosens easily and is less likely than regular masking tape to tear the book board when it is removed.

Paper Towels

Keep paper towels in your work area to wipe glue off your fingers or for quick cleanup.

Pencils

Use a sharpened pencil for accurately marking your paper, book cloth, and book board, as well as for various other measurements. Light pencil marks can also be used to indicate margins when aligning your materials. A white pencil is useful to mark on darker materials.

Plastic Containers

Various containers are useful for holding glues, mixing adhesives, and keeping a damp sponge or cloth away from your materials.

Sandpaper

A small quantity of fine- to medium-grit sandpaper is useful for sanding and smoothing the edges and corners of book board. Sanding is especially effective on boxes and slipcases where the corners may not always line up perfectly after they have been glued together.

Waste Sheets

Waste sheets are loose sheets of scrap paper that are typically used as a surface to glue on and then discard. We primarily use blank newsprint, but any type of waste sheets may be used, including inexpensive copy paper.

Waste sheets can also be used for protecting your book cover when needed, such as when rubbing down decorative papers and book cloth with a bone folder, or simply covering a book or box to offer a layer of protection before placing press boards on top. Blank newsprint is available in pad form in most art supply stores.

The general supplies needed are common household items.

Wax Paper

Wax paper is used as a moisture barrier between the endpaper and the flyleaf of the book while it is drying under weights. We also use wax paper as a release sheet during the construction of boxes and trays. In this case, we typically set the board pieces on a sheet of wax paper after PVA Thick glue has been applied to the edges. After gluing, it is much easier to lift and remove the board pieces off wax paper than off a waste sheet.

BOOKBINDING EQUIPMENT

Bookbinding equipment is a great addition to your studio and certainly will enhance your book and box making experiences. None of the equipment listed in this section is necessary for beginning-level bookbinding. These items are useful to know about, however, should you decide to delve further into book and box making.

A backing press is used for hands-free spine work.

Backing Press*

A backing press is a heavy piece of bookbinding equipment used, among other things, for the process of backing the spine of a book. In advanced bookbinding, after rounding the spine, the text block is placed between the heavy steel jaws and clamped tight. From this position, a hammer is used to form a shoulder along the spine that the cover boards fit snugly against during the casing-in process. Less expensive wooden presses can be adapted for the same purpose.

Board Cutter*

Board cutters, board shears, or board trimmers are specifically designed for cutting book board. The best cutters for this purpose are the old, heavy, cast-iron models that are no longer manufactured and are difficult to find. The one we use in our studio is an 1890s Jacques Board Shear with a 42" cutting blade. New board trimmers are available but are usually of a lesser quality.

A board trimmer is designed for cutting through thick book board.

Book Press*

Book presses are among the most traditional equipment found in bookbinding. They are easy to use and convenient for pressing books and the lids of boxes while they are drying. Antique cast-iron presses are common, but a press with wooden boards is just as effective and not as heavy. For many of our books and boxes we do not use a book press but instead prefer a couple of press boards with several heavy weights of five pounds or more set on top of our finished work. Too much pressure exerted from using a book press can potentially damage a book.

 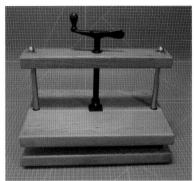

Cast-iron and wood book presses

Finishing Press*

A finishing press is a relatively inexpensive piece of equipment that allows you to position the spine of a book in an upright manner and enables you to work with your hands free. This orientation makes it much easier to apply glue, super, and headbands, as well as perform other steps. A finishing press is especially convenient if you are planning on doing a lot of book repair.

A finishing press allows for hands-free bench work on the spine.

Glue Gun*

An industrial-quality glue gun can be used to quickly glue the trays to the lid in box making. Using a glue gun requires that you be extremely accurate, because the glue dries almost instantly upon contact. If you decide to use a glue gun, we recommend using a high-quality commercial-grade model such as the 3M Polygun TC. Steer away from the inexpensive craft glue guns, since the glue is usually too weak to securely attach trays to the lids of boxes.

A commercial-grade glue gun may be used to glue trays to box lids.

Guillotine*

A hand guillotine is a machine with a large blade that can cut through a large stack of paper to produce a uniform edge. It is traditionally used to trim the head, tail, or fore-edge of a text block before it is cased-in to the covers.

A guillotine is used for trimming a text block.

Paper Cutter*

Most high-quality paper cutters are a worthwhile investment, especially if you are doing a lot of paper cutting. We use several 30" Ingento self-sharpening paper cutters that are made from solid maple for cutting single sheets of paper and book cloth. We do not recommend using a paper cutter for cutting book board, however, as it will dull the blade and damage the cutting-arm mechanism.

A paper cutter with self-sharpening blade

Sewing Cradle*

A sewing cradle is a convenient and inexpensive piece of equipment that allows you to pierce holes on the inside folds of the signatures. It requires that you use a template as a guide for the holes. Place the signature against a stop at one end, along with the template, to ensure that the sewing stations of the signatures are in alignment. A slight opening at the base of the cradle allows space for the awl to cleanly punch through the folded sheets.

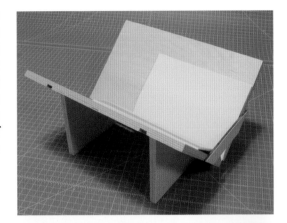

A sewing cradle is used for piercing holes in signatures prior to sewing.

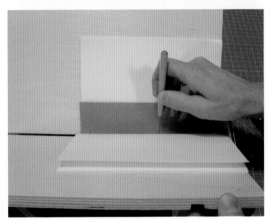

Sewing Frame*

A sewing frame is used for sewing text blocks on tapes or cords. The tapes or cords are then incorporated into the cover of a book to reinforce the attachment of the text block. The crossbar can be adjusted to keep the tape or cords taut during sewing.

A sewing frame keeps tape or cords taut for sewing.

CHAPTER 2

Fundamentals and Methods

This chapter focuses on three fundamentals and related methods that we consider prerequisites for getting started in bookbinding and box making. Let's discuss each, and how they are related to the projects in this book:

1. Understanding and determining grain direction
2. Measuring and cutting your materials
3. Use of adhesives and gluing methods

Common techniques used in traditional bookbinding and box making

UNDERSTANDING AND DETERMINING GRAIN DIRECTION

Before you begin measuring and cutting your materials, one of the first steps in bookbinding and box making is to understand the basics of grain direction. This specifically applies to all decorative papers, text papers, book cloth, and book board. Understanding grain direction helps ensure that your materials are cut and aligned properly. It is key to well-constructed books and box structures.

GRAIN DIRECTION IN PAPER

The grain direction of paper is determined when pulp is moved along a large conveyor belt and the fibers become oriented in the same direction, parallel to the belt. After the paper dries and is cut into different-sized sheets, the grain direction becomes apparent.

The most obvious characteristic of grain direction is that paper folds most easily when it is folded with the grain. This is especially important when folding sheets of text paper into signatures. Folding and creasing the paper along the grain allows the pages to open and close most efficiently. See figs. 2-1 and 2-2.

When the grain runs the long direction in a sheet of paper, we call it grain long. For example, using a standard 8½" × 11" sheet of text paper, grain long would mean the grain runs parallel to the 11" length. When the grain is oriented in the short direction, we call it grain short. If the grain runs short on an 8½" × 11" sheet, it runs parallel to the 8½" direction.

Understanding grain direction in paper is also important when gluing paper to book board. A general rule to follow is to align the grain direction of the paper, or any material, with the grain direction of the book board. Matching the grain direction of both materials will help prevent the board from warping after it dries.

One of the easiest and quickest ways to determine the grain direction of a large sheet of paper is to gently bend a sheet of paper over on itself in both directions. Starting with a large sheet, lightly bend the paper in one direction. Notice the height of the bend, but more importantly feel the resistance it offers. Next, bend the paper in the opposite direction. Again, note the difference in the height of the bend and the resistance you feel in this direction. From this simple test you can usually see and feel that the grain runs parallel with the direction that exhibits the least amount of bend and the least resistance. See figs. 2-3 and 2-4.

There are other ways for determining the grain direction of most commercial or Western papers. One method is to simply tear a small piece of the paper in each direction. Paper torn along the grain will tear in a relatively smooth and straight line. When torn against the grain, the tear line will appear more uneven and

jagged. Another test for determining grain direction is to dampen the paper with a damp cloth or sponge. If the paper has a noticeable grain, the paper will curl parallel to the grain direction. See fig. 2-5.

Note: "Western" papers refer to historical European-based production methods and raw materials used in the process of paper making. The most common materials include flax, hemp, and cotton. "Eastern" or "Oriental" papers refer to a different production method and the use of fibers such as kozo or gampi.

Fig. 2-1. Fold with grain direction of text paper for least resistance.

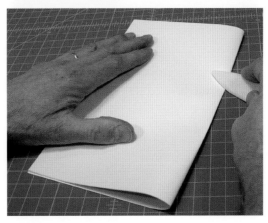

Fig. 2-2. A smoother crease is evident when grain runs parallel to the fold.

Fig. 2-3. (bottom left) Test for grain direction by lightly bending paper in one direction and then noting height and resistance at fold.

Fig. 2-4. (bottom center) Bend paper in the other direction and note height and resistance at fold.

Fig. 2-5. Dampened commercial paper curls parallel to grain direction.

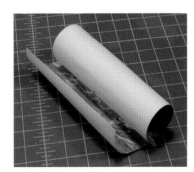

Grain direction is not always evident in handmade papers and many commercial Eastern papers. It is difficult to discern grain direction of handmade papers because they are produced by repeatedly shaking the pulp on a large mould. This results in a more random orientation of the fibers and hence little or no obvious grain direction. Japanese and other Eastern papers that use kozo or gampi exhibit minimal grain direction after a sheet is produced.

PAPER STRETCH

Paper stretch can be an important component to consider when working with Western papers. Paper stretches perpendicular to the grain after it is dampened or glued. The direction of the stretch will increase the dimension of the paper up to ⅛" and sometimes more, depending on the size of the sheet. This dimension change may affect the fit of the paper on the board. Eastern papers do not stretch due to the nature of the fiber used.

If a piece needs to fit exactly, the paper may need to be trimmed before attaching it. In the projects, this may be evident on the inside cover of the slipcase, where the paper turn-in may stretch farther than the book cloth turn-in. You may want to remeasure and trim the paper after first using a sponge to relax and stretch it.

GRAIN DIRECTION IN BOOK BOARD

Book board also exhibits a grain direction because it is formed in the same manner as commercial papers. However, the grain may be less obvious because of the board's thickness. To determine the grain in book board, you can use the same general bending test. Gently flex the book board in both directions and notice that there is greater resistance in one direction than the other. As with paper, the direction that exhibits the least resistance is the grain direction. To illustrate this, we cut two pieces the same size, with one grain short and the other grain long. See figs. 2-6 and 2-7.

Understanding grain direction with book board is important for bookbinding and box making. As much as possible, you want to cut your board pieces with grain long because it produces a more solid structure. A good general

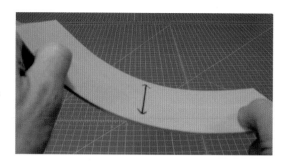

Fig. 2-6. Notice resistance when bending book board with grain, as indicated by arrow.

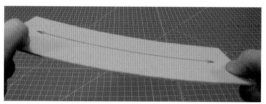

Fig. 2-7. Notice resistance when bending against grain, as indicated by arrow.

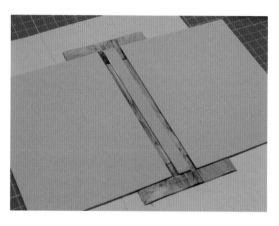

Fig. 2-8. Grain runs long on spine as well as on covers of books.

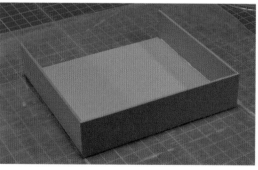

Fig. 2-9. Board pieces for boxes cut grain long produce stronger structures.

rule to follow is that grain should run long or in the same direction as the spine of books. For cutting the strongest walls when making trays of boxes, the grain direction always runs long. See figs. 2-8 and 2-9.

It is also worth noting that grain direction will affect the cutting of book board. You will find it more difficult to cut through book board when cutting against the grain than with the grain. Be prepared to make several additional passes with a heavy-duty knife when cutting through book board against the grain.

GRAIN DIRECTION IN BOOK CLOTH

Book cloth exhibits grain direction that is determined by other factors than paper's, such as thread count and whether the fabric has been backed with paper. Grain direction in starched book cloth is sometimes less perceptible than in paper. However, it is still evident and should be considered when constructing books and boxes. When determining the grain direction of book cloth without a paper backing, follow the same basic bending test as for paper and note the bend and resistance.

When using a book cloth that is backed with paper, however, the bend-and-resistance test is more effective when you place the fabric to the outside and the paper backing on the inside. This allows you to test the grain of the paper, which is the more dominant material when determining the grain direction. See fig. 2-10.

Fig. 2-10. Test paper-backed book cloth with paper backing on inside.

BREAKING THE RULES

Knowing and understanding the grain direction of your materials is an important first step in making books and boxes. As described above, there are several standard rules regarding grain direction that should be considered. However, there are situations and conditions in bookbinding and box making when we break the rules and decide to go against the grain!

One example is opting to fold text paper against the grain when we make a single-signature pamphlet book. In most cases, folding text paper against the grain stresses the fibers and can create a bulky text block. It can also cause the pages to warp in the book. However, with the pamphlet book project, since you are folding only a few sheets, the impact is slight. Also, because the grain direction for most standard 8½" × 11" paper is long, your options for purchasing grain short paper might be limited. See fig. 2-11.

Another instance might be an aesthetic consideration. Sometimes the design on a decorative paper suggests that the paper be placed on a book or box cover in a certain direction. In our work we use a lot of decorative papers with design elements that do not always correspond to the grain direction. In these cases, we recommend placing the paper according to your preference rather than aligning it with the grain direction of the book board. See fig. 2-12.

Fig. 2-11. Text pages in a pamphlet book may be folded against grain.

Fig. 2-12. Image applied to cover without consideration of grain direction

MEASURING AND CUTTING YOUR MATERIALS

A major component of bookbinding and box making is measuring and cutting your materials to the exact size needed. There is no better adage that applies to bookbinding and box making than "Measure twice, cut once. Measure once, cut twice!" For the most accuracy in measuring and cutting, we recommend the following items. See fig. 2-13.

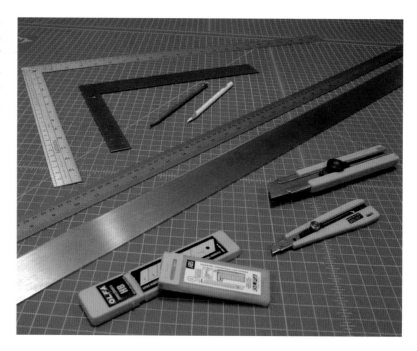

Fig. 2-13. Tools used for measuring and cutting materials

THE MATERIALS

Large Cutting Mat

A cutting mat measuring at least 18" × 24" or larger is recommended. This size is ideal for measuring and cutting large sheets of book board, paper, and book cloth. Look for a cutting mat with ⅛" ruled markings. When using a cutting mat with ⅛" increments, you can still cut a measurement to ¹⁄₁₆" by equally splitting the distance between the grid lines when aligning your materials.

Note: there will be a few measurements that fall between ¹⁄₁₆" calibrations and will need to be measured to ¹⁄₃₂". When this occurs in the projects and if this much precision is required, instead of showing a measurement such as 7²⁵⁄₃₂", we will sometimes round up or down to the nearest ¹⁄₁₆" and insert a (+) or (–) after the measurement, indicating to add or subtract ¹⁄₃₂". For example, instead of 7²⁵⁄₃₂", the instructions will show the measurement as 7³⁄₄(+)".

Metal Rulers

We suggest obtaining several metal rulers with ¹⁄₁₆" calibrations that extend all the way to the edges of the ruler. Metal rulers are used primarily for measuring but can also be used as a straightedge for cutting paper and book cloth on your cutting mat. The two lengths you'll need most are 12" and 36".

Heavy Steel Cutting Bar

A heavy steel cutting bar is far superior to using a thin metal or aluminum ruler, especially when cutting through thick book board. The stability of a heavy bar will prevent it from slipping and make your cutting much safer. A 24" or 36" length cutting bar is most useful.

Carpenter's/L Square

The primary purpose of using a carpenter's or L square is to check the book board pieces for squareness. Simply align the cut board against the two inside edges for a quick visual check. For checking that your board is cut square, this type of tool is much more efficient and accurate than using the grid on your cutting mat.

Heavy-Duty Cutting Knife

A utility knife can be used for cutting book board. Be sure to have plenty of replacement blades. We also recommend heavy-duty knives with break-off blades, such as an Olfa or X-Acto.

Light-Duty Cutting Knife

Light-duty knives are used primarily for cutting paper and book cloth. Olfa or X-Acto knives with replaceable blades or knives with break-off blades are also typically used for this purpose.

Pencil

A sharpened or mechanical pencil is useful for marking your materials. We suggest, in addition to a graphite pencil, that you have a white pencil handy for marking on darker materials.

GETTING STARTED WITH MEASURING AND CUTTING

When getting started with measuring and cutting your materials, plan by grouping your materials in a way that allows you to make as few measurements and cuts as needed. Grouping them together on the basis of what they will be used for will also make it easier to find them when needed. As you proceed, it is helpful to lightly mark on the back what piece you just cut. Be sure to keep in mind the grain direction of your materials before you start cutting.

As much as possible, we use the grid on the cutting mat for quick and accurate measuring. If you do not have a grid, you will need to measure and mark a pattern on the back of your paper and book cloth. When using a grid, align two square edges of the material on two perpendicular grid lines. If your cutting mat has a 0" marking along both the vertical and horizontal axes, square your material along these two lines. See fig. 2-14.

Before you begin cutting, you can also use the grid to quickly square your materials. To square a piece, first place one cut edge along a grid line. If the piece is not square, the perpendicular edges will not run parallel to those grid lines. Keeping the first edge parallel, trim the perpendicular edge so that it is square to the nearest grid line.

Fig. 2-14. Use grid on a cutting mat for quick and accurate measuring.

CUTTING PAPER AND BOOK CLOTH

If you are new to cutting and using a cutting mat, start with a light-duty knife and practice cutting through several waste sheets. Thinner materials such as paper and book cloth should be cut first, rather than starting with the thicker and more difficult book board. You will also want to practice cutting book board to get a sense of the thickness of the material and using a heavy-duty cutting knife.

Set up at a large, sturdy table or workbench and place your cutting mat in a comfortable working position. Align a straightedge across the material so that the ruled measurements on the grid of the cutting mat are visible on either side of the material.

Stand at the workbench while you cut. This will enable you to apply the maximum amount of pressure along the straightedge to keep it stable and prevent shifting. Begin the cutting stroke with your arm extended and drawing the blade toward you. Throughout the stroke, apply firm downward pressure on the straightedge with one hand while applying firm pressure with the knife in your other hand. At the same time, you will also need to maintain pressure with the knife against the straightedge to prevent it from slipping off your straightedge. See fig. 2-15.

All cuts should be done slowly and with enough pressure to cut through the paper or book cloth without needing to make a second pass. To ensure that your first attempt has cut through your material completely, before lifting your hand off the straightedge, check that the material can be pulled away from the cut line. If the paper cannot be removed, proceed with a second cut, using the knife. Cut slightly beyond the end of your measurement in both directions to ensure a clean cut at the corners. For long cuts over 10" or more, it is helpful to shift or "walk" your fingers down the straightedge as you are cutting. By doing this every few inches or so, you can maintain firm pressure on the straightedge along the entire length of the cut.

Remember to replace your blades as soon as they start to dull. This will be evident if you notice a gradual increase in the pressure required to obtain a clean cut or if you are not easily cutting through the paper or cloth on your first attempt.

CUTTING BOOK BOARD

As you might imagine, cutting through book board, even with a heavy-duty knife, is a lot more difficult than cutting paper or book cloth. Blades will need to be replaced frequently for the best results, as well as for safety reasons. In addition, as mentioned above, you will need a heavy steel straightedge for cutting book board. See fig. 2-16.

Unlike cutting paper or book cloth, the goal of cutting book board should not be to cut through the entire board with one cut. Begin with a light cutting stroke by merely scratching the surface of the book board. On the second stroke, you should add a little more pressure and cut only slightly deeper. With the third stroke, apply still more pressure. The deeper you cut into the book board, the more pressure you can apply, since the blade will remain in the cutting channel.

Fig. 2-15. Stand and apply firm downward pressure on straightedge to prevent slipping.

Fig. 2-15 cont.

Fig. 2-16. Use a heavy steel cutting bar and heavy-duty knife when cutting book board.

Depending on the book board's thickness, the amount of pressure applied, and the sharpness of the blade, we have found that it usually takes five or more strokes to cut completely through most medium-weight book board. After cutting the board pieces, check to see if your board is square by setting it against the inside of a carpenter's or L square. See fig. 2-17.

For the beginner, cutting book board can be one of the more challenging skills of bookbinding and box making. We recommend that instead of cutting all the pieces for your project at one time, you cut only the number of pieces needed to complete a section of the project. This gives you a chance to use the pieces and make sure everything is cut and fits together before continuing. Also, from a safety standpoint, it helps limit the amount of cutting you do at any one time.

If you find cutting .090 (³⁄₃₂") book board a little too difficult, consider making your projects with a thinner .060 (¹⁄₁₆") book board. Keep in mind that some of the formulas for making the slipcase and clamshell box will need minor adjustments to accommodate the thinner board, in particular the length measurements of the side walls.

Fig. 2-17. Use a carpenter's or L square to check for squareness.

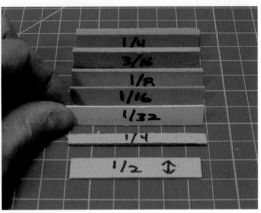

Fig. 2-18. Makeshift measuring guides.

FABRICATING MEASURING GUIDES

We have found that some simple measuring guides are useful when making books and boxes. We fabricate these makeshift tools from book board. Some common sizes are ¹⁄₁₆", ¹⁄₈", ³⁄₁₆", ¹⁄₄", and ½". They should all be cut into lengths of 3", with the grain running long for strength. See fig. 2-18.

Measuring guides can be made from any thickness of book board, but we usually make them from two common sizes, .060 (¹⁄₁₆") and .090 (³⁄₃₂"). We will also occasionally use a .030 board, which is ¹⁄₃₂" in thickness. Guides can be made by laminating different thicknesses of board together and then using the edges of these pieces as the guides. For example, gluing two narrow book board pieces of .090 (³⁄₃₂") thickness together will create a spacing guide of ³⁄₁₆" along the edge. Here is how to cut book board to create different sizes of measuring guides.

Recommended Makeshift Measuring Guides

¹⁄₃₂"	Use the edge of one .030 board.
¹⁄₁₆"	Use the edge of one .060 board.
³⁄₃₂"	Use the edge of one .090 board.
¹⁄₈"	Use the edges of two .060 boards glued together.
³⁄₁₆"	Use the edges of two .090 boards glued together or three edges of .060 board.
¹⁄₄"	Use the edges of two .090 board and one edge of .060 board glued together.
½"	Use the cut width of one .060 or .090 board.

CUTTING OR MITERING CORNERS

When constructing books and boxes, there are several types of miters that are commonly used for covering the corners and open edges of book board. The most common miter is a 45° angle cut from the corners, leaving a space of approximately ⅛" (or 1½ times the thickness of the book board) between the corner and the cut line. Using a ⅛" measuring guide may be helpful for beginners to ensure that this cut is accurately measured. See fig. 2-19.

Other types of miters and cuts include "V" shapes, such as on the outside bottom of boxes and various tab cuts, which allow you to cover the inside corners of boxes and the open edges of trays. These cuts are covered in more detail in the related project chapters. The goal of mitering corners is to create a minimum of overlapping paper or book cloth to result in a neatly covered corner or edge. Mastering a variety of the unique cuts specific to bookbinding and box making is one of the trademarks of professional craftsmanship among bookbinders. See fig. 2-20.

Trimming Book Cloth on Book Board

Before adding decorative paper to the cover of a book or lid, you may need to square the book cloth to the fore-edge of the covers. If this is necessary, measure from the fore-edge of the case or lid to the front edge of the book cloth at the head and tail and on both sides of the case or lid. Note the largest measurement and mark the book cloth to indicate where to place the decorative paper. The measurement should be made so it comes just over the book cloth. See fig. 2-21.

A spring divider is a quick and easy way to mark these measurements. Set the divider by using a ruler and mark the distance from the fore-edge by pressing the point of the divider into the book cloth at the head and tail and on both sides of the case or lid. See fig. 2-22.

Using a light-duty knife, trim the book cloth directly on the board, using a straightedge so both sides of the cover are an equal distance from the fore-edge. See fig. 2-23.

To remove the excess book cloth, make a small diagonal cut in the center of the trimmed piece of book cloth. Lift and peel it from the book board. When removing the book cloth,

Fig. 2-19. Use scissors to make a mitered corner at a 45° angle.

Fig. 2-19 cont.

Fig. 2-20. Neatly mitered corner on a book cover.

Fig. 2-21. Measure from fore-edge to mark placement of decorative paper.

Fig. 2-22. Use spring divider for quick and more-precise measurements.

Fig. 2-23. Trim book cloth on board to an even margin.

you will need to continue your cut over the edges of the book board and onto the inside covers. Line up the straightedge to these cuts on the inside of the case or lid and continue the cut with the knife. Lift and peel the excess book cloth.

ADHESIVES AND GLUING METHODS

This section introduces some of the most commonly used adhesives for bookbinding and box making, along with some of the pros and cons of each. In addition, we will go over a few favorite gluing methods and tips that are helpful for navigating the projects.

PVA

The most popular adhesive available for bookbinding and box making is PVA (polyvinyl acetate). PVA is a synthetic product formulated as a fairly standard white glue. PVA that is specifically designed for bookbinding is nontoxic and generally of a higher quality than other forms. It is quick drying, is archival, has a long shelf life, is nonyellowing, and retains a high degree of flexibility. PVA is also water soluble, which makes it easy to clean up.

The drawbacks of using PVA are important to recognize. Among them is that PVA is quick drying and requires you to work faster than you might like. It is a nonreversible adhesive and, therefore, difficult to undo after gluing. It is also important to be aware that if PVA accidentally gets onto the "good" side of your

Adhesives typically used for bookbinding

paper or book cloth, it will leave a clear, glossy stain when it dries.

Although PVA is an excellent glue to use straight from the bottle, it is helpful to know that it can be thinned or thickened to increase its effectiveness. If PVA is a little too thick, it can be diluted with water to allow it to spread more easily. Evaporation will often lead to PVA thickening over the course of even just a couple of hours, so if you prefer your glue thicker, leave it uncovered for a while. We suggest that when adding water to PVA, you add no more than 5%.

A better alternative to adding water is to add methyl cellulose to PVA, which not only dilutes it but also extends the drying time. See below for more detail on this option.

PVA Thick

PVA also comes in a much more concentrated form, which we call PVA Thick. A similar product is Tacky Glue. Its composition does not mix well with water, and therefore it cannot easily be diluted like regular PVA. PVA Thick dries quickly, which makes it helpful for box making, especially when gluing box walls together. Because of the quick-drying nature of PVA Thick, take care to work at an appropriate pace so the glue does not dry before you are finished. Using only small amounts at a time and keeping the lid tightly on the container will help preserve the shelf life of PVA Thick.

The consistency of PVA Thick can make it difficult to apply with a brush. Therefore, we like to use a makeshift applicator to apply it to the board edges, as well as a makeshift scraper to remove the excess when gluing box walls together. Both are made by using .060 book board and are cut to a size of ½" × 3", with grain running long for added strength. To create the scraper, we simply cut one end at a 45° angle and leave a ⅛" straight edge at the tip to collect the excess glue. See figs. 2-24, 2-25, and 2-26.

Other common uses for PVA Thick are for tipping in endpapers, gluing text blocks and spine reinforcement material along the spine, and for small gluing touch-ups. Along with a thick glue applicator, we use a small natural-bristle brush for tipping in endpapers, a finger for coating the spine with thick glue, and a micro spatula for quick gluing touch-ups.

Fig. 2-24. Thick glue applicator and scraper

Fig. 2-25. Apply PVA Thick with applicator.

Fig. 2-26. Remove excess glue with scraper.

Methyl Cellulose

By itself, methyl cellulose is a weak adhesive, but it is a favorite additive to mix with PVA. The major benefit of adding methyl cellulose to PVA is that it extends the drying time. Without methyl cellulose, PVA dries so quickly that within seconds paper or book cloth can become difficult to shift or remove after being glued down. Adding methyl cellulose also enables PVA to spread more easily. Another benefit to mixing PVA with methyl cellulose is that your brush does not dry out or stiffen as quickly when it is not in use.

Methyl cellulose comes in a powder form and can be mixed in varying concentrations, depending on your preference. We prefer to mix one tablespoon of powder to one pint of warm water. This produces a relatively thin methyl cellulose consistency, which we like because it helps dilute PVA to our preferred viscosity yet helps extend the drying time. See fig. 2-27.

Wheat Paste and Other Natural Adhesives

There are several other bookbinding adhesives, known as natural adhesives, often used in traditional bookbinding. One of the most popular is precooked wheat paste. Wheat paste comes in a powder and is simply mixed with cold water. Other similar adhesives, such as rice starch, require cooking on a stove or in a microwave. See fig. 2-28.

One advantage of using this group of natural adhesives is that they are slow drying. They also can be added to PVA to extend the drying time, much like methyl cellulose. Pastes and starches, unlike PVA, will not cause a glue stain if they accidentally get on the "good side" of your materials. Simply brush any light residue off the material after it dries. Another feature is that unlike PVA, the natural adhesives are reversible, which is appreciated by those involved in book repair and paper conservation.

The major disadvantages of natural adhesives are that they need to be prepared in advance and their drying time is relatively slow. It usually takes twenty-four hours before they are completely dry, as opposed to just several hours for PVA. Another drawback of the natural adhesives is that they have a very short shelf life in the workshop and after just a few days become moldy and unusable. Refrigeration prolongs their usability to about a week. Once the adhesive is applied to the material and dries, there is no concern for mold.

SELECTING BRUSHES

For gluing, we recommend using a good-quality, natural hog bristle brush. See fig. 2-29. Unlike synthetic bristles, natural bristles have an appropriate degree of stiffness for working with bookbinding glues. A high-quality brush that

Fig. 2-27. Methyl cellulose added to PVA increases drying time.

Fig. 2-28. Natural glues come as powder and must be mixed with water.

is properly cared for will last for years. When washing brushes, we recommend using warm water and soap. Be sure to avoid letting brushes dry out with glue left in them, which makes them difficult to clean afterwards.

Personal preference dictates whether to use a round or flat brush. Traditional bookbinder's brushes are round and hold more glue than flat brushes, which is a major advantage

Fig. 2-29. Natural-bristle brushes are preferred for bookbinding.

when gluing large areas. However, a flat brush is easier for beginners to handle, and there are quite a few more size options available. We recommend having several different sizes of brushes. A good starting point is to have two or three natural-bristle artist brushes, which are traditionally used for oil or acrylic painting, in ½" and 1" widths and adding a ¼" brush for small touch-ups.

GLUING TECHNIQUES

The best general advice for gluing is to use brushstrokes that move away from the center of your material and out toward the edges. This will prevent you from overgluing initially at the edges, with the glue then seeping back under your paper or book cloth. Glue on a waste sheet as needed, firmly holding the piece you are gluing to prevent it from shifting. This will ensure that you do not let the piece slip on the waste sheet and accidentally get glue on the "good" side of the material. See figs. 2-30 and 2-31.

Glue should be spread evenly. Try to avoid overgluing, especially when regluing a small area. After gluing, check to make sure you did not miss any spots. As you glue, it is typical to shift your fingers when holding the paper or book cloth. Be sure to add a little dab of glue on those areas where a thin spot of glue may otherwise result.

We recommend using blank newsprint as a waste sheet when gluing, but almost any clean sheet of paper will suffice. When gluing is completed, carefully remove the waste sheet and discard it off the workbench to prevent it from accidentally getting onto your work in progress. At first, removing these waste sheets may seem awkward, but the process of quickly removing them soon becomes efficient and automatic.

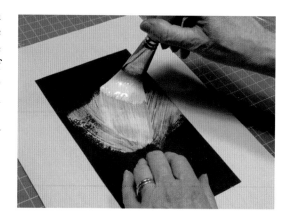

Fig. 2-30. Begin gluing from center and move toward outside edges.

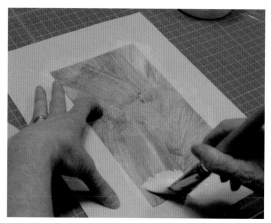

Fig. 2-31. Hold paper firmly to prevent slipping onto waste sheet glue.

CURLING AND PREVENTING WRINKLES

A common occurrence with most machine-made papers is that they curl noticeably when glue is initially applied. If you find that a paper curls excessively, use a dampened sponge or cloth to coat the back of the paper. Wait several seconds until the moisture has helped stretch the paper fibers and you observe the paper begin to "relax." You can then apply glue without worrying about further curling or wrinkling. See fig. 2-32.

Some book cloths will curl after being glued. Unfortunately, dampening book cloth is not an

Fig. 2-32. Dampen commercial paper and wait for it to "relax."

effective solution for curl prevention. In these cases, extra care in gluing and applying book cloth to book board may be required.

One technique to avoid excessive curling in book cloth is to glue the book board first and then place it on the book cloth. Once the board is in place, the book cloth will stay stable, and the board provides something to hold down as you continue gluing. See figs. 2-33 and 2-34.

However, it is important to note that gluing book board first and applying it to materials in this manner will work only when using book cloth or handmade or most Eastern papers. Many Western papers will wrinkle if you attempt to apply book board directly to them without dampening them first and allowing them to stretch as described above.

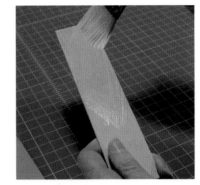

Fig. 2-33. Glue book board first, then adhere to book cloth.

Fig. 2-34. Use book board to keep book cloth stable while gluing.

PLACING GLUED MATERIALS UNDER WEIGHTS

Usually the final step in bookbinding and box making is to place your finished work under pressing boards and weights and to allow it to dry completely. This helps ensure that the freshly glued book boards dry flat and remain flat. See fig. 2-35.

During the drying process, the glued materials will begin to contract or shrink. This is what can sometimes cause the book board to warp. Properly weighting the materials, in addition to allowing enough drying time, usually from overnight to a couple of days, will help eliminate or minimize book board warping.

Fig. 2-35. Place book board under weights overnight to prevent warping.

CHAPTER 3

The Pamphlet Book

The first project is a pamphlet book, sometimes referred to as a single-signature book or booklet. It is an ideal structure to learn as an introduction to bookbinding. It offers beginners a simple, traditional sewing style that, with its exposed stitch, expresses a book art quality.

The number of sheets or folios in a pamphlet book varies, but usually it ranges from two to ten. When folded into a signature format, the result is a book that can contain from eight to forty pages or more. See figs. 3-1 and 3-2.

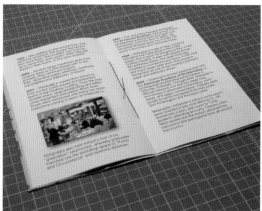

Fig. 3-1. Completed pamphlet books with sewing visible along spine

Fig. 3-2. Open pamphlet book with finishing knot on inside of spine

The pamphlet book is a popular structure for printing a short story, biography, collection of poems, artwork, or invitations. It is also a fun collaborative project for writing classes. A popular trademark of a pamphlet book is that it is a nonadhesive binding, meaning that no gluing is needed to complete the structure.

The instructions are for making a pamphlet book that utilizes three sheets of text paper, a flyleaf, and a heavy decorative paper for the outside cover. The text paper is a standard sheet size of 8½" × 11". The flyleaf is a separate sheet of decorative paper. The outside cover utilizes an 8⅝" × 19¼" cover-weight paper that is folded inward at the fore-edges, giving the book a more finished appearance. These five sheets, when folded together into a single signature, result in a twenty-page pamphlet book.

This project uses an 8½" × 11" text paper for the text pages, because it is readily available and easy to send through a printer. The one caveat is that most text paper of this size is grain long, so there is more resistance when folding the sheets. Although grain short would be ideal, since this is a beginning-level project and is a relatively thin pamphlet book, using 8½" × 11" text paper with grain long is a practical option.

To prepare your materials for the project, proceed to cut the materials with the dimensions as listed below. Refer to the measuring and cutting instructions in chapter 2, "Fundamentals and Methods." Formulas for making custom-size pamphlet books are listed in chapter 8, "Book and Box Making Formulas."

MATERIALS, TOOLS, AND SUPPLIES

Fig. 3-3. Materials, tools, and supplies needed to complete pamphlet book

Materials

Decorative cover paper
Flyleaf
Sewing thread
Text pages

Tools and Supplies

Awl
Bone folder
Cutting knife (light duty)
Cutting mat
Metal ruler
Pencil
Scissors
Sewing needle
Weight

PROJECT MATERIALS, DIMENSIONS, GRAIN DIRECTION, AND QUANTITIES

Keep in mind that the measurements listed, and the materials and other aspects of this project, can be adjusted in infinite combinations to create unique pamphlet books. As you increase your skills, you may want to experiment. See fig. 3-3.

Materials	Dimensions	Grain Direction	Quantity
Decorative Papers			
Cover Paper	8⅝" × 19¼"	Short or Long	(1)
Flyleaf	8½" × 11⅛"	Short or Long	(1)
Text Pages			
Text Paper	8½" × 11"	Short or Long	(3)
Thread			
Thread	24"	N/A	N/A

PART I. PREPARE THE SINGLE SIGNATURE FOR SEWING

Step 1

Begin by using three sheets (folios) of text paper that measure 8½" × 11". The sheets can be printed or left blank. Jog the sheets together and then neatly fold them in half so that it produces a twelve-page, 5½" × 8½" section. Use a bone folder to make a tight crease along the fold. See fig. 3-4.

Fig. 3-4. Fold text paper and use bone folder to create a tight crease.

Step 2

Fold the flyleaf in half in the same manner and use the bone folder to crease the fold. Insert the text pages inside the folded flyleaf to create a four-folio or sixteen-page signature. We recommend cutting the flyleaf slightly wider than the text paper at 8½" × 11⅛". The extra width of the flyleaf will cover the slight fanning of the text pages along the fore-edge. See fig. 3-5.

Fig. 3-5. Fold flyleaf in half and place text pages inside.

Step 3

After folding the oversize decorative paper cover in half, use the bone folder to create a sharp crease along the fold. The larger-size paper, 8⅝" × 19¼", will later be turned in to protect the text pages at the fore-edge. The added ⅛" at the head and tail also serves to protect the text pages. See figs. 3-6 and 3-7.

As an alternative, a smaller outside cover may be used as described in part IV, "Pamphlet Book Options."

Fig. 3-6. Fold oversize sheet of decorative paper cover in half.

Fig. 3-7. Use bone folder to make sharp crease.

Step 4

Insert the folded edge of the flyleaf with text pages against the inside fold of the decorative cover paper. Align it so that the signature is recessed from the head and tail of the cover to produce a $\frac{1}{16}$" protective margin on each side. See fig. 3-8.

The fore-edge of the decorative cover will extend approximately 4" from the fore-edge of the text pages and flyleaves.

Fig. 3-8. Insert flyleaf, with text pages against inside fold of decorative cover.

Step 5

Open the decorative cover paper and signature to the center fold. Set a ruler just below the fold line and measure to the center of the text pages. Mark the center sewing station at 4¼". From that point, the distance to measure in both directions is flexible, but for this project we measured 2¼". Mark a sewing station at the tail of the pamphlet book at 2" and one at the head of the booklet at 6½". See fig. 3-9.

Fig. 3-9. Mark three sewing stations along inside fold of signature.

Step 6

Using a thin paper awl, pierce through the fold at each of the three sewing stations. As the awl begins to penetrate each mark, close the cover and look for the point of the awl to come through precisely on the outside fold. See figs. 3-10 and 3-11.

Fig. 3-10. Insert a thin awl through fold of signature.

Fig. 3-11. Point of awl should pierce through fold to outside.

PART II.
SEW THE PAMPHLET BOOK

The steps that follow are for sewing an "in and out" figure-eight pattern. The starting point is from the inside center of the pamphlet, and it ends in a finishing knot, also at the inside center. If you prefer the finishing knot on the outside of the spine, you will need to start the sewing process from the outside of the cover. This allows you to tie the finishing knot on the outside and is described in part IV, "Pamphlet Book Options."

Step 1

Determine the amount of thread required to sew a single signature by measuring a length of sewing thread against the length of the spine. The length should equal 2½ times the length of the spine. For the exposed stitch of the pamphlet book, we chose a thick and heavily waxed four-ply thread, but an unwaxed thread is suitable. See fig. 3-12.

To help stabilize the booklet while sewing, it is helpful to hold the signature in place by using a small weight on the inside of the pamphlet.

Fig. 3-12. Calculate length of thread needed for sewing a single signature.

Step 2

To pass the thread through the smaller eye of the needle, it may be necessary to flatten the end with the tip of a bone folder. After threading the needle, leave about a 2" tail. See figs. 3-13 and 3-14.

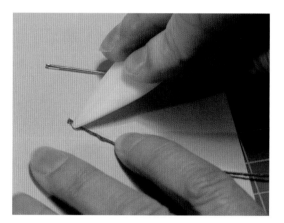

Fig. 3-13. Flatten end of waxed thread with tip of bone folder.

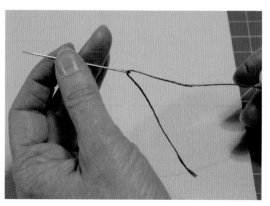

Fig. 3-14. Thread needle and leave 2" tail.

Step 3

Begin sewing the pamphlet stitch from the inside of the signature at the center or second sewing station. See fig. 3-15.

Insert the needle into the hole and pull through the signature, to the outside of the cover, leaving approximately a 3" tail of thread on the inside of the book. See fig. 3-16.

Fig. 3-15. Insert sewing needle in sewing station at center of signature.

Fig. 3-16. Pull thread through to outside cover, leaving 3" tail on inside.

Step 4

Once on the outside of the spine, enter the sewing station at the first sewing station or tail of the signature by passing the needle from the outside of the cover back to the inside. See fig. 3-17.

As you pull the needle through to the inside of the fold, check along the outside cover and make sure the thread stays taut along the spine. See fig. 3-18.

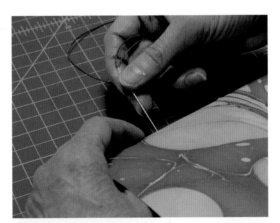

Fig. 3-17. Insert needle from outside of spine through first sewing station.

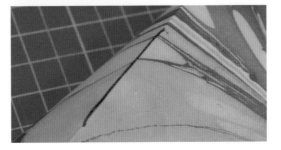

Fig. 3-18. Check thread along spine to make sure it is snug.

Step 5

From the first sewing station inside the signature, bring the thread past the sewing station in the center and exit the needle at the third station at the head of the signature. See fig. 3-19.

As you bring the needle through the hole, the thread should tighten along the inside fold and sit snugly over the 3" tail piece at the center sewing station. See fig. 3-20.

Fig. 3-19. Bypass second (center) sewing station and exit at third sewing station.

Fig. 3-20. Pull thread taut over second sewing station.

Step 6

Reenter the second or center sewing station from the outside spine and back into the same hole you came out of to begin sewing. In the process of reentering the hole, be careful to not pierce through the thread on the outside or inside of the hole. See fig. 3-21.

Pull the thread taut as you reenter to the inside. See fig. 3-22.

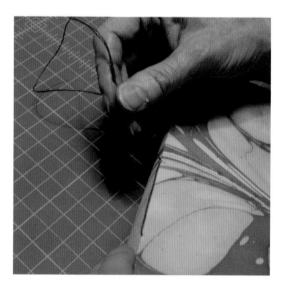

Fig. 3-21. Reenter through center sewing station.

Fig. 3-22. Pull thread taut on outside of spine.

Step 7

Once back on the inside of the signature, position the thread attached to the needle on one side of the spine thread lying in the fold. Position the loose end that was created at the start of the sewing process on the other side of the thread. Tie the two ends around the thread along the spine and make a double knot to hold the three pieces of thread together in the center of the book. See fig. 3-23.

Fig. 3-23. Tie a knot around thread running from station 1 to station 3.

Use scissors to trim the two loose ends of thread to approximately ½" and complete the pamphlet stitch on the inside of the spine. See fig. 3-24.

Fig. 3-24. Cut thread, leaving two ½" tails at knot.

PART III.
COMPLETE THE COVER OF
THE PAMPHLET BOOK

Pamphlet book before turning in outside covers

Step 1

With the single-signature sewing now completed, open the front cover so you are viewing the inside portion of the back cover extending beyond the flyleaf and text pages.

Place a thin metal ruler or straightedge under the flyleaf so that ¹⁄₁₆" of the ruler is exposed at the fore-edge of the flyleaf. See figs. 3-25 and 3-26.

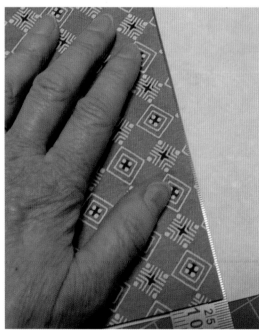

Fig. 3-25. Place straightedge under flyleaf so that ¹⁄₁₆" is exposed.

Fig. 3-26. Close-up of straightedge placement under flyleaf

Step 2

Using the pointed end of the bone folder, place it against the straightedge and use firm pressure to score the back-cover paper. This additional small margin for the cover will help protect the interior flyleaf and text pages. It also adds a more finished fore-edge to the pamphlet book (fig. 3-27).

Fig. 3-27. Score cover paper along straight-edge with bone folder.

Turn in the cover paper along the scored line and use the bone folder to make a sharp crease along the fold (fig. 3-28).

Fig. 3-28. Turn in cover along score line and crease folded edge.

Step 3

Repeat the same process in steps 1 and 2 on the front side of the cover so that both front and back are turned in at the fore-edges, completing your pamphlet book (fig. 3-29).

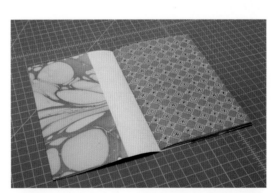

Fig. 3-29. Repeat same process on other side.

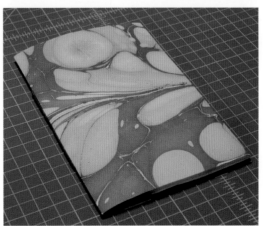

The completed Pamphlet Book Project

PART IV.
PAMPHLET BOOK OPTIONS

Basic Cover

A simpler cover option may be used instead of an oversize decorative cover paper and flyleaf. Cut a cover paper ⅛" to ¼" longer than the length of the text pages, to just cover the fanning at the fore-edge (figs. 3-30 and 3-31).

Fig. 3-30. Invitation with basic paper cover

Fig. 3-31. The three-hole stitch with shortened spacing keeps it simple yet elegant.

Finishing Knot on the Outside

If you would prefer the finishing knot on the outside of the spine, start the sewing with the needle at the outside, center sewing station (figs. 3-32 and 3-33).

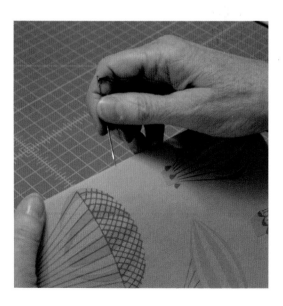

Fig. 3-32. Start needle at outside center sewing station for finishing knot on outside.

Fig. 3-33. Knot on outside of spine adds a decorative element to pamphlet book.

Five-Hole Pamphlet Book

As an alternative to the three-hole pamphlet book, two additional sewing stations can be added. The first sewing station is still marked at the center or third sewing station of the signature, but the holes are each spaced 1½" apart, for a total of five sewing stations.

The sewing remains a figure-eight pattern, and as with the three-hole style, you bypass the center station. The example starts and finishes on the outside of the spine. Start at the center (or the third) sewing station on the outside along the spine and sew the following in-and-out pattern:

1. Begin sewing from the outside.
2. Enter at the center station.
3. Exit at the second station.
4. Enter at the first station.
5. Reexit at the second station.
6. Enter at the fourth station, skipping the center station.
7. Exit at the fifth station.
8. Reenter at the fourth station.
9. Reexit at the center station (fig. 3-34).
10. Finish by tying knot on the outside (figs. 3-35 and 3-36).

Fig. 3-34. Reexit at center sewing station from inside to outside.

Fig. 3-35. Five-hole pamphlet book with sewing starting and finishing outside spine

Fig. 3-36. Spine view of completed five-hole sewing

CHAPTER 4

The Flat-Back Book

The flat-back book is considered one of the most basic structures in traditional bookbinding. The use of a flat board spine gives the book a solid and well-defined hinge. The multiple-signature sewing style is typical for this type of binding and is significantly more developed than the pamphlet stitch.

The flat-back book is typically used for thinner books. The page count varies, depending on the thickness of the paper, but generally flat-backs contain fifty to one hundred pages and are ¼" to ½" in terms of thickness. The instructions that follow are for using fifteen sheets of 7" × 11" text paper (grain short), producing a book with sixty (front and back) pages. For the pictured project, we used a high-quality, medium-weight text paper (80 lb. / 115 gsm).

Depending on the weight of the text paper you select, the thickness of your completed text block may be different from the measurements in this project. Therefore, it will be important to measure for the spine thickness separately after your text block is completed. If you choose to use standard 8½" × 11" text paper, you will need to use the formulas found in chapter 8, "Book and Box Making Formulas," to determine the measurements for cutting your materials.

Completed flat-back book. We preprinted the pages for this project.

MATERIALS, TOOLS, AND SUPPLIES

Materials

Beeswax
Book board (.090 or ³⁄₃₂" thickness)
Book cloth
Decorative paper
Endpaper
Headbands
PVA
PVA Thick
Sewing thread
Super
Text pages

Tools

Bone folder
Cutting knives
Cutting mat
Glue brushes
Joint rods
Makeshift tools (measuring guides)
Press boards
Ruler
Scissors
Sewing needle
Spring divider
Square
Weights

Supplies

Damp cloth
Paper towels
Pencil
Sponge
Waste sheets
Wax paper

PROJECT MATERIALS, DIMENSIONS, GRAIN DIRECTION, AND QUANTITIES

Remember that the measurements listed, and the materials and other aspects of this project, can be adjusted in infinite combinations to create your own unique flat-back books. As you increase your skills, you may want to experiment.

Materials	Dimensions	Grain Direction	Quantity
Book Board			
Book Covers	5½" × 7¼"	Long	(2)
Spine *	⁹⁄₁₆" × 7¼"	Long	(1)

* You will need to measure the exact thickness of your completed text block plus the thickness of two book boards to determine the width measurement of the spine. The width measurement with board was ⁹⁄₁₆".

Materials	Dimensions	Grain Direction	Quantity
Decorative Paper			
Book Covers	4⅞" × 8¾"	Long	(2)
Endpapers	7" × 11"	Short	(2)
Book Cloth			
Spine	4¼" × 8¾"	Long	(1)
Spine Materials			
Super	2⅞" × 6½"	Not Applicable	(1)
Headbands	⅞"	Not Applicable	(2)
Text Pages			
Text Paper (80 lb. / 115 gsm)	7" × 11"	Short	(15 sheets)

PART I.
PREPARE THE TEXT BLOCK
FOR SEWING

Step 1

For this project, count out fifteen sheets (folios) of a medium-weight text paper measuring 7" × 11". The sheets can be printed or left blank. The grain of the paper should run short. Divide the fifteen sheets into five signatures of three sheets each (fig. 4-1).

For this project we started with 8½" × 11" paper, and after formatting and printing, trimmed the sheets to 7" × 11". All project measurements are based on these dimensions. Jog each set of sheets to square them and fold them in half so that the signatures measure 5½" × 7". Use the bone folder along the folded edge to create a sharp crease (fig. 4-2).

Fig. 4-1. Five sets of three sheets each for signatures

Fig. 4-2. Make a sharp crease with bone folder.

Step 2

After the five signatures are folded, jog them together along the head, tail, and spine so that the pages are square and aligned as evenly as possible along the three edges. DO NOT jog them along the fore-edge. Place the stack of signatures with the folds facing you, and the fore-edge pointing away. Set a heavy weight on the stack to compress the signatures and prevent them from shifting. Position the weight so that it is recessed slightly from the folded edges along the spine (fig. 4-3).

Fig. 4-3. Use a weight to stabilize text block.

Step 3

Mark the sewing stations using a ½" wide measuring guide, ruler, or grid lines on a cutting mat. We describe making a ½" measuring guide in chapter 2, "Fundamentals and Methods." We use this makeshift tool for most signature markings.

To mark the first sewing station, place the ½" guide along the outside edge of the text block. The guide should be positioned at a 90° angle so that one long edge is flush with the edge of the text block, and the other edge is recessed ½" from the tail of the spine. With a sharp pencil, draw a straight line against the inside of the measuring guide from the bottom signature to the top signature (fig. 4-4).

When the measuring guide is removed, a small tick mark should be evident along the five folds. Repeat this same step at the opposite end of the text block so that you have two sets of sewing stations marked on the spine and both are recessed ½" from the head and tail.

From these two sets of marks, move the measuring guide 1½" toward the center of the signatures. Draw two sets of tick marks at each location on both sides of the ½" wide measuring guide. This will add four additional sewing stations along the spine. When completed, six sets of tick marks on all five signatures should be clearly marked (fig. 4-5).

Fig. 4-4. Mark signatures along folds.

Fig. 4-5. Text block marked with six sewing stations

Step 4

One final set of tick marks should be added to your signatures. This set, however, should be marked at only one end of the text block. Place your measuring guide at a slight angle and just to the outside of the first sewing station. Draw a line so that each tick mark is slightly offset from the other. These marks are NOT sewing stations. The offset reference marks help you quickly see if one of the signatures is placed out of sequence (figs. 4-6 and 4-7).

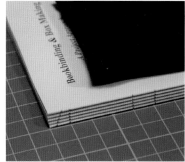

Fig. 4-6. Draw an angled line as a set of reference marks.

Fig. 4-7. Angled reference line to prevent signatures from being placed out of order

Step 5

Using a thin paper awl or bookbinder's awl, pierce holes through all six sewing stations of each signature, from the outside to the inside along the folds. This is accomplished by placing a set of folded sheets at the edge of a workbench, with the pages open and the fold just over the edge of the bench (fig 4-8).

Penetrate the entire folded signature in a straight line that is perpendicular to the fold. The point of the awl should exit directly along the interior of each fold (fig. 4-9).

After you pierce the six sewing stations, turn the signature over and begin to stack in reverse order. Be sure not to pierce the reference marks.

Fig. 4-8. Pierce holes at each sewing station from outside to inside.

Fig. 4-9. Piercings should be on fold line on inside of signatures.

PART II.
SEW THE TEXT BLOCK

Step 1

To determine the amount of thread required to sew all the signatures, measure your sewing thread against the height of the text block. Count the number of signatures and add one additional length to arrive at how many lengths are required for sewing the text block. Since the project uses five signatures, the total lengths of thread needed is six (fig. 4-10).

Fig. 4-10. Measure length of thread needed for five signatures.

Step 2

Before threading the needle to start sewing, we recommend waxing the thread with a small amount of beeswax. Adding a coat of beeswax helps prevent the thread from tangling and adds a little tack to prevent it from slipping. Place the thread over the wax, with your thumb on top, and pull the complete length of thread over the beeswax several times (fig. 4-11).

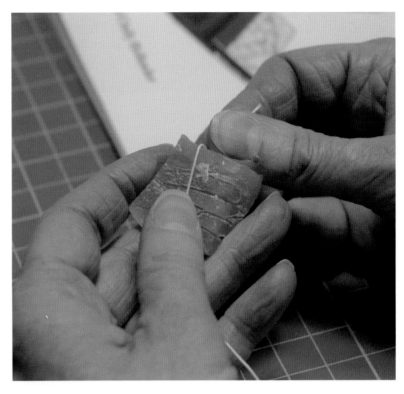

Fig. 4-11. Wax the thread prior to sewing.

Step 3

Begin by threading the needle and leaving a 2" tail at the eye. Pick up the first signature and bring the needle though the first sewing station at the tail, beginning on the outside of the fold and proceeding to the inside (fig. 4-12).

Continue to pull the thread through the hole until approximately a 2" tail remains on the outside of the folded signature (fig. 4-13).

Fig. 4-12. Begin sewing on outside of first signature.

Fig. 4-13. Leave a 2" tail.

Step 4

With the needle now on the inside, bring it to the outside of the fold, through the second sewing station. Proceed back "in" through the third sewing station and "out" through the fourth (fig. 4-14).

Sew a final "in and out" pattern through the fifth and sixth sewing stations, exiting the needle on the outside of the fold at the sixth sewing station. Throughout the entire sewing process, it is important to make sure the thread has been pulled taut. While holding on to the tail, pull the thread parallel to the fold of the signature (fig. 4-15).

Fig. 4-14. Sew an "in and out" pattern along fold.

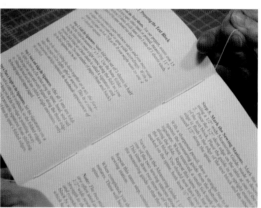

Fig. 4-15. Pull thread taut as you proceed.

Step 5

Pick up the second signature and place it behind the first. At the same time, open the second signature slightly so you can grasp both the closed first signature and the opened second signature together with one hand (fig. 4-16).

Insert the needle in the sixth sewing station at the head of the second signature and pull the thread through to draw the two signatures together. This is called a "cross-over stitch" and is used to connect the end of one signature to the beginning of the next. The stitch should be snug, but not so tight that one of the signatures rides up over the other (fig. 4-17).

Fig. 4-16. Add second signature behind first.

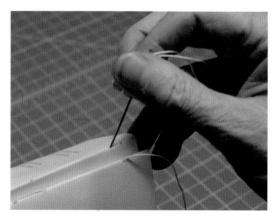

Fig. 4-17. Connect signatures, using cross-over stitch.

Step 6

After the cross-over stitch is completed, exit through the fifth sewing station. Before entering the fourth station, you will use a "link stitch" between two sewing stations. Place the needle under the thread between the fourth and fifth sewing stations of the first signature, point it toward the fourth sewing station, and pull the thread through (fig. 4-18).

Proceed to enter the fourth sewing station of the second signature and pull the thread snug, creating an "X" pattern between the first and second signatures. This link stitch is used to reduce the slack in the thread and lock the signatures together, adding stability to any set of paired sewing stations along the spine (fig. 4-19).

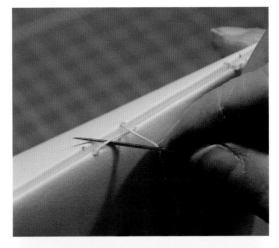

Fig. 4-18. Begin first "link stitch" on first signature.

Fig. 4-19. Insert needle into sewing station after making link stitch.

Step 7

Exit through the third sewing station, link under the thread at the paired second and third sewing stations on the first signature, then enter the signature at the second sewing station. After completing the two link stitches along the spine, exit the needle and thread at the first sewing station of the second signature (fig. 4-20).

Tie the 2" tail of thread at the first signature to the sewing thread in a double or square knot, linking the two signatures at the first sewing station (fig. 4-21).

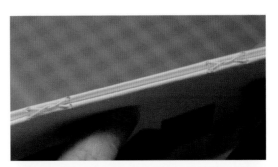

Fig. 4-20. Link stitches connecting first and second signatures.

Fig. 4-21. Lock first two signatures with double knot.

Step 8

Continue the sewing process by adding the third signature behind the second signature. The first and second signatures should be closed and the third signature open as you are holding them together. Begin with the same cross-over stitch by entering the first sewing station and exiting at the second (fig. 4-22).

However, before you enter the third station, link-stitch by inserting the needle under the thread on the second signature, which is closest to the third station of the third signature. You will make a link stitch before entering the fifth sewing station of the third signature as well (fig. 4-23).

Fig. 4-22. Add third signature behind second and connect with cross-over stitch.

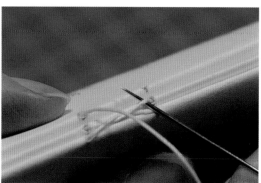

Fig. 4-23. Link stitch between two sewing stations.

Step 9

Once you arrive at the end of the third signature, you will need to attach the second and third signatures together, using a "kettle stitch." The kettle stitch will alternate with the cross-over stitch at the end of every other signature to lock all subsequent signatures to the text block. Begin the kettle stitch by inserting the needle under the cross-over stitch thread between the first and second signatures at the sixth sewing station (fig. 4-24a).

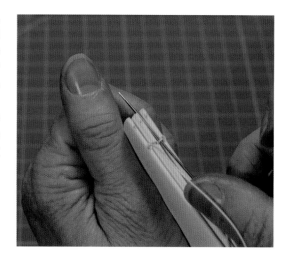

Fig. 4-24a. Start kettle stitch by passing needle under cross-over stitch.

As the needle passes outside the head of the text block, pull just enough thread through to form a ½" loop (fig. 4-24b).

Next, bring the needle back around to where you started and through the loop in the same direction. The second time it passes through, however, pull the thread all the way to form a knot and lock the second and third signatures together (fig. 4-24c).

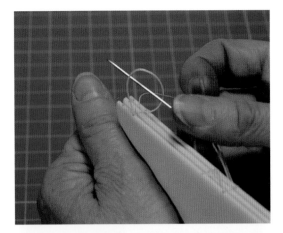

Fig. 4-24b. Create a ½" loop and then go back through loop.

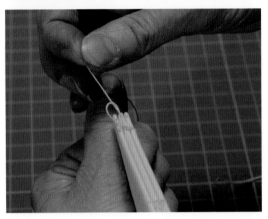

Fig. 4-24c. Pull to knot and complete kettle stitch.

Step 10

Continue adding the fourth and fifth signatures as in steps 8 and 9. After the five signatures have been sewn and at the completion of the final signature, make a double kettle stitch between the last two signatures. This is done by simply repeating the kettle stitch twice to firmly lock the final signature (fig. 4-25).

Trim the excess thread by using scissors at the head and tail of the text block. Both ends should be cut to a length of approximately ½" (fig. 4-26).

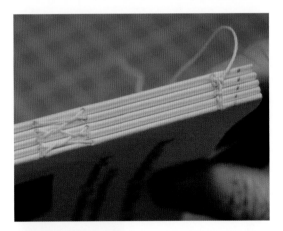

Fig. 4-25. Tie a double kettle stitch after all five signatures have been completed.

Fig. 4-26. Trim thread at head and tail to ½".

PART III.
GLUE AND COMPLETE
THE TEXT BLOCK

Step 1

To prepare the spine of the text block for gluing, jog the signatures once again so that they are square across the spine, as well as along the head and tail. To keep the text block stable, place one of the two book boards for the case under the text block, and position the spine so it extends over the front edge of the board by no more than ⅛".

In addition, position the book board so that it is flush with the edge of the workbench, and the text block now is extending over the edge of the workbench. Place the second cover board on top of the text block, also recessed ⅛". Set a 3 to 5 lb. weight on top of the board. The book board and the weight will assist in compressing the folds of the signatures along the length of the text block (fig. 4-27).

Fig. 4-27. Position text block just over edge of workbench.

Step 2

Remove a small amount of PVA Thick glue from the bottle and, using your finger instead of a brush, apply thick glue along the spine. Bend down or kneel so you are at eye level and looking directly at the spine as you apply the glue. This will enable you to apply glue between all the open spaces between the folds of the signatures (fig. 4-28).

The heavy weight, along with additional downward hand pressure, will ensure that the signatures do not shift during the gluing process. Apply a thin coat and wipe off any excess glue, using a clean finger. When completed, allow the glue to dry for at least ten minutes before attaching the endpapers (fig. 4-29).

Fig. 4-28. Apply PVA Thick along spine.

Fig. 4-29. Cover all open space between signatures.

Step 3

Before attaching the endpapers to the front and back of the text block, fold them in half, with the "good side," or the sides that you want visible upon opening the book, folded inward. Use the bone folder to make a sharp crease along the fold (fig. 4-30).

The portion of the endpaper that gets tipped on to the text block is called the flyleaf, and it becomes the first and last "leaves" of the text block. The portion of the endpaper that is glued to the front and back cover boards and is used to attach the text block to the case is called the pastedown.

Fig. 4-30. Fold endpapers and crease with bone folder.

Step 4

To assist you in gluing the endpaper, use a waste sheet that has been folded lengthwise to create a narrow, masked edge. Place the folded waste sheet between $\frac{1}{16}$" and no greater than $\frac{1}{8}$" from the edge of the folded endpaper (fig. 4-31).

Using PVA Thick, brush a narrow strip of glue along the folded edge of the endpaper. Hold the folded waste sheet firmly in place on top of the flyleaf, with a second waste sheet underneath (fig. 4-32).

Fig. 4-31. Mask a narrow strip along fold with waste sheet.

Fig. 4-32. Hold mask firmly in place when applying glue.

Step 5

When gluing is completed, carefully remove the waste sheet to reveal a thin and neatly glued line of PVA Thick along the folded edge of the endpaper (fig. 4-33).

Turn the glued endpaper over and place it along the spine of the text block. This process is called "tipping-in." The folded edge should be carefully lined up, parallel along the length of the spine edge and even with the head and tail of the text block. Press down firmly, using the bone folder to ensure good contact (fig. 4-34).

Repeat this step on the other side of the text block to tip-in the second endpaper.

Fig. 4-33. Glue shown along folded edge of endpaper

Fig. 4-34. Tip-in by aligning folded edge along fold of first signature.

Step 6

To apply super (spine reinforcement) to the spine, fold it lengthwise and pinch the super just at the head and tail to mark the midpoints. With scissors, snip a very small "V" shape at each crease, creating two notches to help identify the center along the length of the super (figs. 4-35 and 4-36).

Fig. 4-35. Snip a very small "V" shape at center top and bottom of super.

Fig. 4-36. Notch in super indicates midpoint for centering on spine.

Before attaching the super, apply a light coat of PVA Thick, using your finger along the length of the spine of the text block so it becomes tacky. Then, using the two notches as a reference, place the super on the spine so that it is centered and recessed evenly, ½" from both the head and tail (fig. 4-37).

Approximately 1" of the super should overhang on both sides along the length of the spine for later attachment to the cover boards. Apply a second coat of PVA Thick to the spine, being careful not to overglue. Work the glue through the mesh until the super feels securely attached.

Fig. 4-37. Add coat of PVA Thick; first along spine, then over super.

Step 7

Decorative headbands should be two equal pieces, both approximately ¾" or slightly wider than the thickness of the spine. Before gluing the headbands in position, check that the fabric portion below the decorative bead will sit just above the sewing stations at the head and tail and not over them. Trim the fabric so that it sits just above the sewing, to reduce bulk along the spine.

Apply a small amount of PVA Thick across the spine, just slightly below the top edge at the head and tail of the text block. Recessing the glue will allow for some oozing after the headbands are pressed onto the spine (fig. 4-38).

Attach headbands both to the head and the tail so that only the narrow decorative bead is visible above the text block. Keep in mind that the front of the headband should be facing the fore-edge of the book (fig. 4-39).

After placing the headband in position, check to ensure that the decorative bead is parallel along the top edge of the text block. If the headband is not aligned evenly at this point, remove and reattach it; otherwise the unevenness will be noticeable after casing-in the text block. Allow the headbands to dry for a few minutes. Then carefully trim each side with sharp scissors to the exact width of the spine (fig. 4-40).

To prevent the threads of the headband bead from unraveling, dab a very small amount of glue on the two cut edges of the headband bead, as seen in fig. 4-41.

Fig. 4-38. Dab small amount of glue at head and tail for attaching headband.

Fig. 4-39. Ensure that bead of headband is parallel along top of text block.

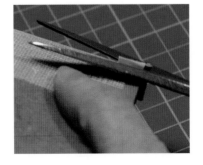

Fig. 4-40. Carefully trim headbands flush with width of text block.

Fig. 4-41. Dab PVA Thick to headband ends to prevent unraveling.

PART IV.
CONSTRUCT THE CASE
FOR THE TEXT BLOCK

Step 1

The measurements for the book boards of the case are determined by the height and width measurements of the text block. For the flat-back book project, the text block measures 5½" × 7". The board width is cut the same as the width of the text block. For the height, ¼" is added. As a result, the measurements for the book boards are 5½" × 7¼".

To measure the width of the spine, you will need to carefully determine the thickness of the text block, plus the thickness of the two board covers. A quick and simple way to measure the required spine width is to place the two cover boards over the text block. Slightly squeeze the boards together and measure the spine thickness with a ruler. We usually measure to ⅟₃₂" when determining the width measurement for the spine (fig. 4-42).

Once the width measurement is determined, cut the spine board. The height of the spine is the same height as the cover boards. For the project, the spine board measurement was ⁹⁄₁₆" × 7¼", but your width measurement may be different, depending on the thickness of your text block.

Fig. 4-42. Measure spine and book board thickness.

Step 2

Position the book cloth so that the side to be glued is facing up. Using a ruler or a spring divider, accurately find the midpoint across the width at the head and tail of the book cloth. Draw a light pencil line running the length of the book cloth spine piece (fig. 4-43).

In addition, accurately mark the center of the spine board at the top and bottom with a pencil to line it up with the centerline on the book cloth. Apply PVA to the spine board and place it on the book cloth, lining it up precisely with the two sets of lines. The spine board should also be centered so that there is an equal margin for the turn-in at the head and tail of the book cloth (figs. 4-44 and 4-45).

Fig. 4-43. Find midpoint of book cloth.

Fig. 4-44. Apply PVA to spine board piece.

Fig. 4-45. Center spine board on book cloth spine.

Step 3

Create a pair of ¼" spine-spacing guides. See the measuring guide instructions in chapter 2. These spacing guides will help you quickly measure the ¼" gap between the spine board and the cover boards. This important gap produces the hinge or joint for the book covers. A ruler can also be used to measure the required ¼" gap; however, spacing guides ensure that there is always exact and consistent spacing (fig. 4-46).

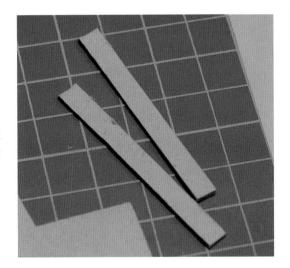

Fig. 4-46. Create ¼" spine-spacing guides.

Step 4

Apply glue to one side of the book cloth, up to the spine board piece. Remove the waste sheet. Then place the two ¼" measuring guides directly against the edges of the spine at the head and tail, with the ends of the guides resting off the book cloth (fig. 4-47).

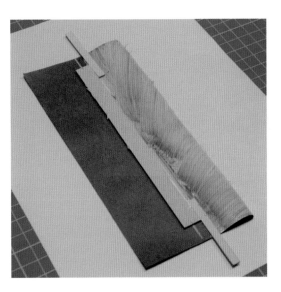

Fig. 4-47. Place spacers on cloth next to spine board.

Set one of the cover boards against the two spacing guides, as in fig. 4-48.

Fig. 4-48. Place book board cover against measuring guides.

Make sure the cover board and spine board are aligned at the head and tail, then quickly remove the guides to prevent them from getting stuck. Once the guides are removed, the spine gap should be an even ¼" along the length of the spine. Repeat this step, attaching the second cover board to the other side of the spine (fig. 4-49).

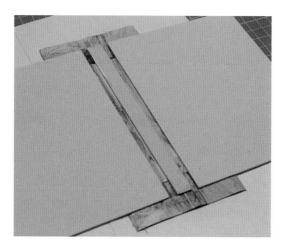

Fig. 4-49. Attach second cover board to spine.

Step 5

Apply glue to the book cloth at the head and tail, being careful to not overglue. Turn in the book cloth at one end and press down onto the inside of the spine and cover boards. Be sure the book cloth is kept snug along the edges of the board as you turn in the cloth (fig. 4-50).

Use the bone folder to assist you in pressing the book cloth into the gap between the spine and cover boards, to ensure there is good contact along the spine hinge or joints (fig. 4-51).

Turn the cover over and gently use your thumb along the spine gap so that there is good contact on the outer side of the book cloth, and to help define the outside and inside edges of the two joints (fig. 4-52).

Fig. 4-50. Turn in book cloth at head and tail.

Fig. 4-51. Use bone folder to ensure good contact in joint.

Fig. 4-52. Use thumb to form hinge on outside of spine cloth.

Step 6

After the case is made, we like to check the fit of the text block in the case to make sure that when the spine of the text block is placed tightly against the spine of the case, there is a ⅛" margin at the fore-edge. There should also be a ⅛" margin along the head and tail. In addition, the headband should sit parallel along the head and tail of the text block as well as at the head and tail of the spine board of the case (fig. 4-53).

Although on occasion you may need to remake the case if it does not fit properly, it is better to catch the problem now before attaching the decorative papers and beginning the casing-in process.

Fig. 4-53. Test the text block in the case.

Step 7

Before adding the decorative papers, you may need to square the book cloth to the fore-edge of the covers. See chapter 2 if you need to trim the book cloth to an even margin. To determine even placement of the decorative paper, measure from the fore-edge of the case to the front edge of the book cloth at the head and tail and on both sides of the case. In the project, we used a measurement of 4¼" from the fore-edge to where it just overlaps the book cloth by ¼". We used a white pencil with a sharp point to mark on the dark book cloth (figs. 4-54 and 4-55).

Fig. 4-54. Mark placement of decorative paper.

Fig. 4-55. Marks on book cloth spine at four points

As an option, a spring divider is a quick and easy way to make these measurements. Check your measurement against a ruler. Set the divider to 4¼" by using a ruler, and simply mark the distance from the fore-edge by pressing the point of the divider into the book cloth at the head and tail on both sides of the case. These four equal measurements will be used as guides for the placement of the decorative paper (figs. 4-56 and 4-57).

Fig. 4-56. Use a spring divider with a ruler.

Fig. 4-57. Transfer measurement to book cloth.

Step 8

It is helpful to place the case in a closed and angled position before attaching the paper to the cover. Apply glue to one of the cover pieces of decorative paper (fig. 4-58).

Then carefully place the spine edge of the paper so it is just concealing the marks on the book cloth and remains parallel to the spine. The turn-ins of the head, tail, and fore-edge all should be an even margin of approximately ⅝" (fig. 4-59).

Fig. 4-58. Apply glue to decorative paper.

Fig. 4-59. Attach paper by placing over marks on book cloth.

Step 9

After positioning the decorative paper, miter the two outside corners by using scissors. The cuts should be at a 45° angle, leaving a space from the corner to the cut line of approximately ⅛", or 1½ times the thickness of the book board (figs. 4-60 and 4-61).

It is always safer to have a little more margin than less, so a mitered cut that is cut twice the thickness from the corner is recommended. You can also use a ⅛" measuring guide to ensure that this cut is accurate.

Fig. 4-60. Miter corner by using scissors.

Fig. 4-61. Corners mitered at 45° angle

Step 10

After both corners have been mitered, turn in the two short sides at the head and tail of the cover board and press down onto the inside of the cover. If at any point the glue appears to be drying after making the mitered cuts, lightly reglue the turn-ins.

At both mitered corners along the short edge, make a slight tuck by using the bone folder before turning in the fore-edge. This downward and slightly inward tuck is important for eliminating a small burr from forming at the corners (fig. 4-62).

Fig. 4-62. Turn in short side and use bone folder to tuck in corners.

Step 11

After the tuck, bring the turn-in over the fore-edge of the board and press down onto the inside of the cover (fig. 4-63).

Use the bone folder to tap or apply firm pressure at all four corners of the completed case, to remove any burrs or sharpness (fig. 4-64).

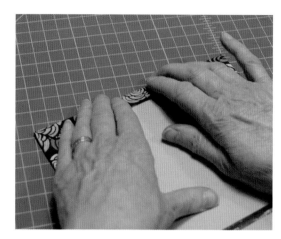

Fig. 4-63. Turn in fore-edge.

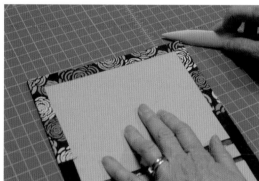

Fig. 4-64. Tap corners to gently round them.

Step 12

Repeat steps 7 through 11 on the other cover to complete the attachment of the second decorative paper. After both sides of the case are covered, carefully smooth out the papers, making sure there are no wrinkles or air pockets. Avoid using the bone folder to rub directly on the paper. Instead, use your fingers. If you do use a bone folder, place a protective waste sheet over the paper beforehand. The case is now completed (fig. 4-65).

Fig. 4-65. Completed flat-back case

PART V.
CASE-IN THE TEXT BLOCK

Step 1

Insert the text block in the case and make sure that the spine of the text block is pressed firmly against the spine board. There should be no gap. In addition, visually check the margin at the fore-edge and at the head and tail. These margins should be square and approximately ⅛" (figs. 4-66 and 4-67).

Fig. 4-66. Place text block in case for visual check of spine placement.

Fig. 4-67. Ensure that margins are square at head, tail, and fore-edge.

Step 2

Position the book so that the fore-edge of the text block is facing you and the cover is leaning against a support object at about a 45° angle. Insert a waste sheet between the flyleaf and the pastedown portion of the endpaper. Place it so that it fits snugly against the inside fold (fig. 4-68).

Fig. 4-68. Insert a waste sheet between flyleaf and pastedown.

Lift the super just enough to be able to apply a thin coat of PVA under the spine reinforcement material and onto the pastedown (fig. 4-69).

Fig. 4-69. Brush glue onto pastedown underneath super.

After this initial coat of glue is applied, using your brush, press the super onto the glued portion of the pastedown. Apply a thin coat of glue on top of the super and continue to glue the entire pastedown (figs. 4-70 and 4-71).

Be careful not to apply too much glue at the head and tail near the spine. This will help keep glue from oozing out once the book is cased-in and placed under weights or in a book press. Carefully remove the waste sheet when gluing is completed.

Fig. 4-70. Glue over top of super.

Fig. 4-71. Continue to glue entire pastedown.

Step 3

With the traditional method of casing-in, at this point you would simply close the covers onto the glued pastedown. This process sometimes leaves the pastedowns out of square. We offer an alternative method that helps ensure that the pastedowns are glued square to the covers.

To accomplish a square pastedown, lift up the two outside corners and place them on the inside book cover so that the same visual margin of ⅛" corresponds to what was evident in step 1. This will ensure not only that the spine of the text block remains pressed tightly against the spine of the case, but that the square margin stays intact. Once this alignment occurs, press only the top half of the pastedown onto the board, while keeping the cover in an upright position (fig. 4-72).

Fig. 4-72. Attach top half of pastedown with a ⅛" margin.

Step 4

Next, turn the book 180° so that the book cover is now flat on the table and facing toward you. At the same time, grasp the text block and the back cover and hold it upright. With your one hand in this position, use your other hand to press down the bottom portion of the pastedown, working it slowly toward the spine (fig. 4-73).

Avoid using a bone folder at the spine to prevent accidentally tearing the pastedown at the fold. Using firm pressure with your fingers is enough to help secure the pastedown to the inside cover.

Fig. 4-73. Rotate book 180° and smooth bottom half of pastedown.

Step 5

Place a piece of wax paper, cut slightly larger than the length and width of the text block, between the pastedown and the flyleaf. Close the text block. The wax paper between the pastedown and flyleaf prevents moisture from the glue being absorbed by the flyleaf and first few pages of the text block. Wax paper also ensures that any glue that might seep out as the book is pressed does not damage the text block (fig. 4-74).

Fig. 4-74. Insert wax paper between pastedown and flyleaf.

Step 6

Repeat steps 2 through 5 and glue the second pastedown. Allow for a square ⅛" margin at the fore-edge and along the head and tail, as with the first cover.

As you glue the second pastedown, you may need to close the cover slightly to accurately position the pastedown, because the other side has already been glued to the first cover board and there is less play along the spine (fig. 4-75).

After turning the book cover 180°, as shown in step 4, grasp the cover board along with the text block and keep it at a slightly lower angle as you press the pastedown toward the spine. Since there is less play along the spine, this will help reduce the tension as the second pastedown is attached.

Add a second piece of wax paper between the pastedown and flyleaf when completed.

Fig. 4-75. Pastedown on second cover matching square at head, tail, and fore-edge

Step 7

Use the bone folder to apply even and firm pressure along the two joints between the board covers and the spine on both sides of the case. Firm pressure applied by the bone folder will help ensure tighter contact of the text block to the book cover. It will also help define the joint before the joint rods are placed in position along the hinges (fig. 4-76).

Fig. 4-76. Apply firm pressure along joint, using bone folder.

Step 8

Before placing in a book press or under press boards and weights, add a pair of joint rods. A wire rod thickness of ¹⁄₁₆" (2 mm) is ideal and should be placed directly in the two joints of the book. We use the long, straight bottom portion of a wire clothes hanger as joint rods. A pair of thin knitting needles (size 0) are also a good size for this purpose (fig. 4-77). Although it is not essential to add the wire rods, we have found that it helps define and tighten the joint, giving the book a cleaner look when completed.

Fig. 4-77. Add joint rods at hinge before placing between press boards.

Step 9

Set your completed book between two pressing boards, with a clean waste sheet in between the boards and your book. Be careful to ensure that the wire rods are kept securely in the joints during this process. Place a couple of heavy weights (5 to 10 lbs.) on top of the pressing boards, and allow your book to dry overnight with the wax paper remaining in place.

A book press can be used, but we advise against applying too much pressure, which can cause glue to ooze along the spine (fig. 4-78).

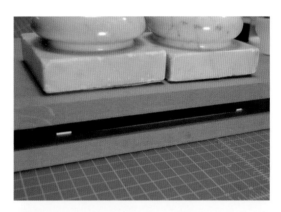

Fig. 4-78. Set book between press boards and add heavy weights.

The completed Flat-Back Book Project

The Round-Back Book

The round-back book is similar in construction to the flat-back but incorporates a more complex and stronger spine structure, allowing it to contain a greater number of signatures. In this chapter you will learn how to form a rounded spine and attach a hollow tube, which allows a thicker text block to open easier. You will also learn how to tie on sewing thread as needed. In addition, we show how to add a decorative trim strip to the covers. Many of the construction steps found in the round-back are the same as for the flat-back project. For clarity, however, the construction of the round-back book is presented as a complete project.

Typically, round-back books are about ¾" or greater in thickness. The instructions call for using forty-eight sheets of 5½" × 10" text paper, producing a book with 192 pages. We used a medium-weight 80 lb. / 115 gsm text paper, which results in a completed text block of approximately 1". Depending on the specific paper you choose, the thickness may vary. Therefore, it is always important to measure the actual thickness of the completed text block to determine the spine width needed. Formulas for making your own custom round-back book are listed in chapter 8.

Completed round-back book

MATERIALS, TOOLS, AND SUPPLIES

PROJECT MATERIALS, DIMENSIONS, GRAIN DIRECTION, AND QUANTITIES

Remember that the measurements listed, and the materials and other aspects of this project, can be adjusted in infinite combinations to create your own unique round-back books. As you increase your skills, you may want to experiment.

Materials

Beeswax
Book board (.090 or ³⁄₃₂" thickness)
Book cloth
Cover-weight paper
Decorative paper
Endpapers
Headbands
Kraft paper
PVA
PVA Thick
Sewing thread
Super (spine reinforcement)
Text pages

Tools

Bone folder
Cutting knives
Cutting mat
Glue brushes
Hammer
Joint (wire) rods
Makeshift tools / measuring guides
Press boards
Ruler/straightedge
Scissors
Sewing needle
Spring divider
Square
Weights

Supplies

Damp cloth
Masking tape
Paper towels
Pencil
Sponge
Waste sheets
Wax paper

Materials	Dimensions	Grain Direction	Quantity
Book Board			
Book Covers	5" × 5¾"	Long	(2)
Decorative Papers			
Book Cover	3¾" × 7¼"	Long	(2)
Trim Strip	¾" × 7¼"	Long	(2)
Endpaper	5½" × 10"	Short	(2)
Book Cloth			
Spine	5½" × 7¼"	Long	(1)
Spine Materials			
Spine Inlay *	1¹⁄₁₆" × 5¾"	Long	(1)
Spine Lining *	¹⁵⁄₁₆" × 4½"	Long	(1)
Hollow Tube *	2¹⁵⁄₁₆" × 5½"	Long	(1)
Super (Spine Reinforcement)	3½" × 5"	Not Applicable	(1)
Headbands	1¼" length	Not Applicable	(2)
Text Pages			
Text Paper	5½" × 10"	Short	(48 sheets)

* You will need to measure the exact thickness of your completed text block to determine the width measurement. The project spine width measurement was 1". See pages 98–99.

PART I.
PREPARE THE TEXT BLOCK
FOR SEWING

Step 1

For the round-back book, count out forty-eight sheets (folios) of a medium-weight text paper measuring 5½" × 10". The sheets can be printed or left blank. The grain of the paper should run the short direction or the same direction as the spine of the book. From those forty-eight sheets, divide them into twelve signatures, with each signature containing four sheets (fig. 5-1).

Jog each set of sheets to square them, then fold them in half so that the signatures measure 5" × 5½". Use the bone folder along the folded edges to create a sharp crease (figs. 5-2 and 5-3).

Fig. 5-1. Twelve sets of four sheets for signatures

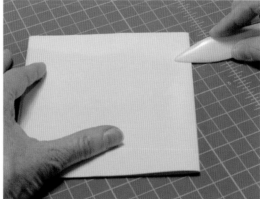

Fig. 5-2. Fold and jog sheets to square signature.

Fig. 5-3. Crease folds sharply with bone folder.

Step 2

After the twelve signatures are folded, jog them together on a flat surface along the head, tail, and spine so that the pages are square and aligned as evenly as possible along the three edges. Do NOT jog them along the fore-edge (fig. 5-4).

Fig. 5-4. Jog signatures along spine to square them for marking.

Keeping the signatures square, stack them so the folds are facing you. To help stabilize the signatures, place a piece of book board on top of the stack so that it is slightly recessed from the signatures' folded edges. Set a heavy weight on the board to help compress the signatures and prevent them from shifting (fig. 5-5).

Fig. 5-5. Stabilize text block with board and weight.

Step 3

Mark the sewing stations by using a ½" wide measuring guide, ruler, or grid lines on a cutting mat. We describe making a ½" measuring guide in chapter 2, "Fundamentals and Methods," and we use this makeshift tool for most of the signature markings.

To mark the first sewing station, place the ½" guide along the outside edge of the text block. The guide should be positioned so that one long edge is flush with the edge of the text block, and the other edge is recessed ½" from the tail of the spine. With a sharp pencil, draw a straight line against the inside of the measuring guide from the bottom signature to the top signature (fig. 5-6).

When the measuring guide is removed, a small tick mark should be visible along each of the twelve folds. Repeat at the head of the text block. You now have two sets of sewing stations marked on the spine edge, each recessed ½" from the head and tail (fig. 5-7).

Fig. 5-6. Mark ½" from tail with set of tick marks along folds.

Fig. 5-7. Sewing stations marked at head and tail

Step 4

From these two sets of marks, move the measuring guide to the center of the signatures. This time draw two sets of tick marks, one on each side of the ½" wide guide. This will add two additional sewing stations along the spine (fig. 5-8).

When completed, you will have four sets of tick marks on all twelve signatures, which will become the four sewing stations (fig. 5-9).

Because of the small spine length of the text block, no additional sewing stations are needed. Generally, individual or pairs of sewing stations should be marked approximately 1½" to 2" apart. If the spine length was 8½", for example, we would add one additional pair of sewing stations, for a total of six sewing stations along the spine. (See an example of six sewing stations in chapter 4, "The Flat-Back Book.")

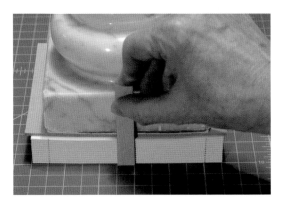

Fig. 5-8. Mark pair of sewing stations at center of spine.

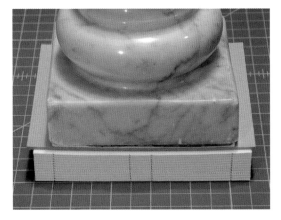

Fig. 5-9. Four sewing stations marked on signatures

Step 5

One final set of tick marks should be added to your signatures. This set should be marked at only one end of the text block. Place your measuring guide at a slight angle, just to the outside of the first sewing station. Draw a line so that each tick mark is slightly offset from the other (fig. 5-10).

This set is NOT a sewing station. Instead, the reference marks help you quickly see if one of the signatures is placed out of sequence or in the wrong direction (fig. 5-11).

Fig. 5-10. Angle-measuring guide to draw reference marks

Fig. 5-11. Text block marked with angled reference line

Step 6

Place the first signature at the edge of your workbench, with the pages open and the folds just over the edge of the bench. Using a thin awl, pierce the sewing-station hole from the outside to the inside of the folds at the first sewing station. Continue this process through all the stations, except for the angled set of reference marks (fig. 5-12).

The awl should penetrate the entire folded signature perpendicular to the fold, and the point of the awl should exit directly along the interior of each fold (fig. 5-13).

After the piercing is completed, turn each signature over and place them in reverse order, one on top of the other. Be sure to maintain the correct sequence of signatures by checking the reference marks along the folds.

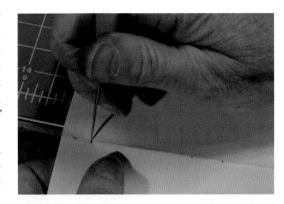

Fig. 5-12. Pierce holes at sewing stations from outside to inside of fold.

Fig. 5-13. Holes should be centered on inside fold of signatures.

PART II.
SEW THE TEXT BLOCK

Step 1

To determine the amount of thread required to sew the entire text block, measure the sewing thread against the spine length or height of the text block. For a larger number of signatures, such as with the round-back, count the number of signatures and add two additional lengths to arrive at how many lengths of thread are required. Since the project uses twelve signatures, the total number of lengths of thread needed is fourteen (fig. 5-14).

Generally, the longest length of thread used for sewing is about an arm and a half's length, or 36" to 48". Because this project requires such a long length of thread, we suggest cutting it in half. You will combine the lengths by "tying on" during the sewing process.

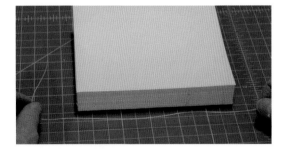

Fig. 5-14. Measure length of thread needed for twelve signatures.

Step 2

Before threading the needle to start sewing, we recommend waxing the thread with a small amount of beeswax. Adding a coat of beeswax helps prevent the thread from tangling and adds tack to prevent it from slipping. Place the thread over the wax, with your thumb on top, and pull the complete length of thread over the beeswax two or three times (fig. 5-15).

Fig. 5-15. Wax the thread prior to sewing.

Step 3

Thread the needle, leaving a 2" tail at the eye. Pick up the first signature and bring the needle through the first sewing station at the tail of the text block. Beginning on the outside of the fold, bring the needle and thread to the inside. Continue to pull the thread through the hole until approximately a 2" tail remains on the outside of the folded signature (fig. 5-16).

Fig. 5-16. Begin sewing from outside of first signature.

Step 4

With the needle now on the inside, bring it back to the outside of the fold through the second sewing station. Proceed back "in" through the third sewing station and "out" through the fourth and last sewing station (fig. 5-17).

Throughout the entire sewing process, it is important to make sure the thread has been pulled taut. While holding on to the tail, pull the thread parallel to the fold of the signature. This ensures that you do not risk tearing the paper at one of the sewing stations by inadvertently pulling the thread upward (fig. 5-18).

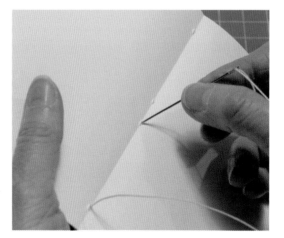

Fig. 5-17. Sew using an "in and out" pattern along signature.

Fig. 5-18. Pull thread taut parallel to spine. There should be no slack in thread.

Step 5

Pick up the second signature and place it behind the first (fig. 5-19).

At the same time, open the second signature slightly so you can grasp both the closed first signature and the opened second signature together with one hand (fig. 5-20).

Insert the needle in the outside of the fourth sewing station of the second signature. Pull the thread through to the inside and draw the two signatures together. This is called a cross-over stitch and is used to connect the end of one signature to the beginning of the next. The stitch should be snug, but not so tight that one of the signatures rides up over the other (fig. 5-21).

Fig. 5-19. Bring second signature behind first.

Fig. 5-20. Second signature lined up with first

Fig. 5-21. Connect two signatures by using cross-over stitch.

Step 6

After the cross-over stitch is completed, you will use a "link stitch" between the second and third stations. First bring the needle from the inside to the outside of the fold at the third sewing station. Next, place the needle under the thread of the first signature and point it toward the second sewing station (fig. 5-22).

Proceed to enter the second sewing station of the second signature and pull the thread snug, creating an "X" pattern between the first and second signatures. This link stitch is used to reduce the slack in the thread and lock the signatures together, adding stability to any set of paired sewing stations along the spine (fig. 5-23).

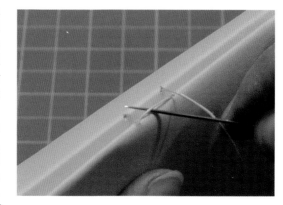

Fig. 5-22. Pass needle under thread on first signature to begin first "link stitch."

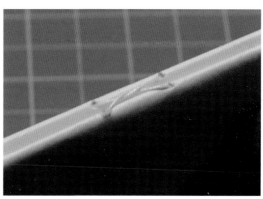

Fig. 5-23. Completed link stitch between stations 2 and 3

Step 7

Complete the second signature by exiting through the first sewing station. Once on the outside of the signature, tie the 2" tail of thread to the sewing thread on the needle in a double or square knot (fig. 5-24).

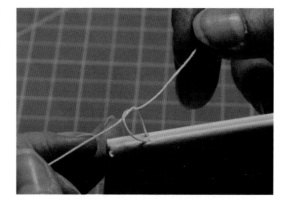

Fig. 5-24. Tie double knot to connect first two signatures.

Step 8

Bring the third signature behind the second signature. Open the third signature slightly and, using one hand, grasp it along with the first two signatures (fig. 5-25).

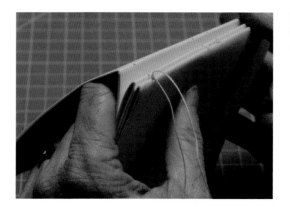

Fig. 5-25. Add third signature with cross-over stitch.

Proceed to sew into the first sewing station and exit at the second sewing station. At this point, you will repeat the link stitch. However, before you enter the third station, bring the needle under the thread of the second signature. Insert the needle between the threads on the side of the link or "X" closest to the sewing station you will be entering (fig. 5-26).

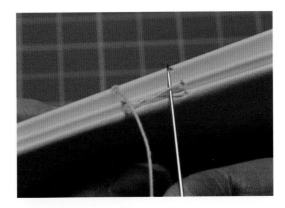

Fig. 5-26. Link under thread closest to hole on third signature.

Step 9

Once you arrive at the end of the third signature, you will need to attach the second and third signatures together using a kettle stitch. The kettle stitch will alternate with the cross-over stitch at the end of every other signature to lock all subsequent signatures to the text block.

Now the needle is on the outside of the third signature. Begin the kettle stitch by passing the needle under the cross-over stitch thread between the first and second signatures at the fourth sewing station (fig. 5-27a).

As the needle passes outside the head of the text block, pull just enough thread through to form a ½" loop, as in fig. 5-27b.

Next, bring the needle back around to where you started and through the loop in the same direction. The second time through, however, pull the thread all the way to form a knot and lock the second and third signatures together (fig. 5-27c).

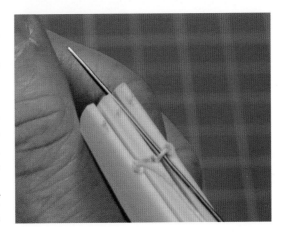

Fig. 5-27a. Start kettle stitch by passing needle under cross-over stitch.

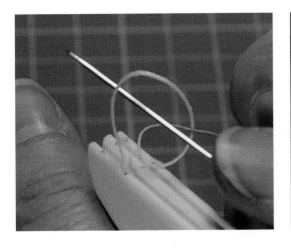

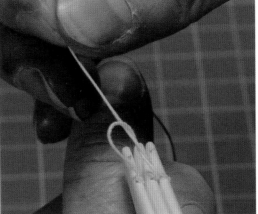

Fig. 5-27b. Create a ½" loop, then bring needle back through loop.

Fig. 5-27c. Pull thread to complete kettle stitch.

Step 10

Sew the fourth signature in the same manner as the third. As you reach the second sewing station, the needle will again enter on the opposite side of the "X" and closest to the hole that the needle is entering (fig. 5-28).

With each signature that is added, the link or the "X" pattern stretches in opposing directions, creating a herringbone sewing pattern (fig. 5-29).

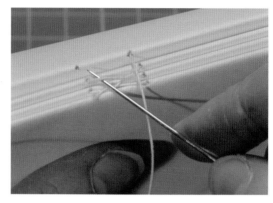

Fig. 5-28. Link under thread closest to hole on fourth signature.

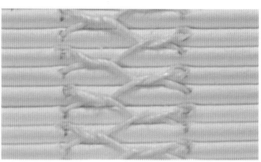

Fig. 5-29. Herringbone sewing pattern that results from link stitch

Step 11

Continue adding signatures in the same manner until you reach about the sixth or seventh signature and you begin to run out of thread. At this point you will need to tie the second length on to the first. This should occur on the inside of the signature and near the midpoint just before the second sewing station or just after the third.

To tie on the new length of thread, using a slip knot, we used two different colors to make it easier to demonstrate the steps (fig. 5-30).

Take the new length of thread and form a ½" loop around your forefinger. Pinch your forefinger and thumb where the threads cross, allowing for about a 3" tail of thread at the bottom (fig. 5-31a).

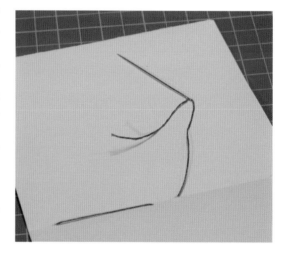

Fig. 5-30. Colored thread to better demonstrate tying-on of additional thread

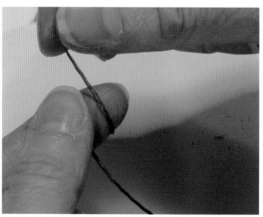

Fig. 5-31a. Form a ½" loop around your forefinger.

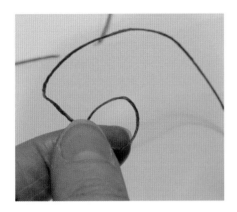

Fig. 5-31b. Slide loop off finger and grasp crossed threads.

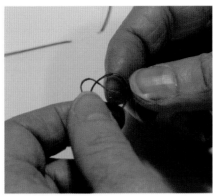

Fig. 5-31c. Form a second loop by inserting the long thread through first loop.

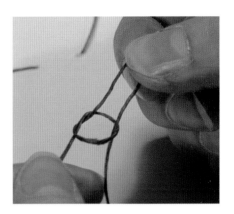

Fig. 5-31d. As you form the second loop, pull it through original loop, forming a slip knot.

Slide the loop off your forefinger while holding on to the crossed threads (see fig. 5-31b). Begin to form a second loop with the long length of thread and insert it back through the original loop (fig. 5-31c).

As you begin to feed the new loop through the original loop, pull it upward to start to form the slip knot. Let go of the loop while continuing to hold on to the tail of the thread. Tighten the knot just enough so it is snug, but do not overtighten (fig. 5-31d).

Pick up the needle with the old thread still attached and slide it through the new loop. Bring the slip knot past the needle and onto the old thread to a point just before the sewing station it came through (fig. 5-32).

To tighten the slip knot around the new thread, pull both the tail end and the rest of the new thread tightly until you feel a snap. If you do not feel a snap, test the knot to make sure it is snug before proceeding. If the knot is not securely fastened, you will need to form another slip knot by repeating these five steps (fig. 5-33).

Fig. 5-32. Feed needle with old thread through slip knot.

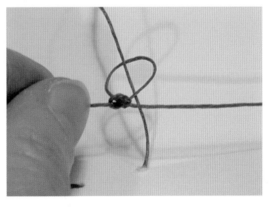

Fig. 5-33. Tighten slip knot until you feel a snap.

Remove the needle from the old thread and rethread onto the new thread. Cut the two short lengths of thread to between ¼" and ½" (fig. 5-34).

Fig. 5-34. Remove needle from old thread and trim.

Tying-on thread is a traditional process in hand bookbinding. The knot on the inside of the signature visually illustrates the book has been hand-sewn (fig. 5-35).

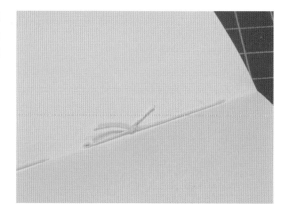

Fig. 5-35. A tie-on is an indication of a hand-sewn text block.

Step 12

Providing you do not run out of thread and need to tie-on again, continue sewing in the same manner as described in steps 8 through 10 until all twelve signatures have been attached. At the completion of the final signature, make a double kettle stitch between the last two signatures. This is done by simply repeating the kettle stitch twice to firmly lock the final signature. Trim the excess thread by using scissors at the head and tail of the text block. Both ends should be cut to a length of approximately ½" (fig. 5-36).

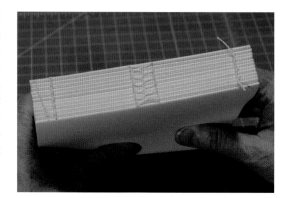

Fig. 5-36. Tie a double kettle stitch to complete sewing of text block.

PART III.
GLUE AND COMPLETE THE
TEXT BLOCK

Step 1

Jog the text block so that it is square across the spine as well as along the head and tail. Place one of the two book boards of the cover under the text block and position the spine so that it extends over the front edge of the board by no more than ⅛".

In addition, position the book board so that it is flush with the edge of the workbench, and the text block is extending over the edge of the workbench no more than ⅛". Place the second cover board on top of the text block, also recessed ⅛", and set a weight of 3 to 5 lbs. on top of the board to stabilize the text block. The book board and the weight will assist in compressing the folds of the signatures along the length of the text block (fig. 5-37).

Fig. 5-37. Position text block just over edge of workbench.

Step 2

Take a small amount of PVA Thick, and using your finger (instead of a brush), apply glue along the spine. Bend down or kneel so you are at eye level and looking directly at the spine as you apply the glue. This will enable you to glue all the open spaces between the folds of the signatures (fig. 5-38).

The heavy weight, along with additional downward hand pressure, will ensure that the signatures do not shift during the gluing process. Apply a thin coat and wipe off any excess glue, using a clean finger. When completed, allow the glue to dry for about ten minutes before rounding the spine. The softer and more malleable the glue, the better for rounding.

Fig. 5-38. Apply PVA Thick along spine.

Step 3

Rounding the spine is an important step for several reasons. Rounding reduces the stress along the spine when the text block is opened, and prevents it from collapsing. It also helps minimize the swelling along the spine caused by the folds and sewing thread. By using light hammering to offset the folds of the signatures, the thickness is reduced so that the spine remains level with the fore-edge. A rounded book also opens easier and lies flatter than one that is not rounded.

To accomplish the rounding process, you will need a medium-weight hammer of approximately 10 to 16 ounces. A hammer with a slightly rounded head is helpful to avoid damaging the folds, but a standard large claw hammer is also adequate for this process.

Set the text block in front of you, with the spine facing away. Grasp the text block firmly, with the thumb of one hand pressing against the fore-edge. At the same time, place your fingers on top of the text block, pulling it toward you as you begin to use the hammer.

Start in the approximate center and middle of the spine, at the sixth or seventh signature, and strike the text block with a light to medium force (fig. 5-39).

As you make contact along the spine, use a glancing blow rather than a direct hit, by quickly lifting the hammer. Shift the position of the hammer along the spine as you proceed so that you make contact along the entire length of the text block.

Turn the book over and repeat until an even arc spanning approximately one-third of a circle is evident. Avoid applying too much direct force with the hammer and damaging the folds. The objective is to stretch the glue and slightly offset each signature from the other (figs. 5-40 and 5-41).

As the rounding process stretches the glue, it also creates a memory. This elastic nature of PVA will allow the spine to flatten and reform into the same rounded position as you work with the text block in future steps.

Fig. 5-39. Start rounding in middle of text block.

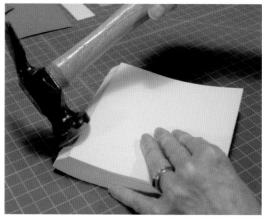

Fig. 5-40. Round spine by offsetting each signature.

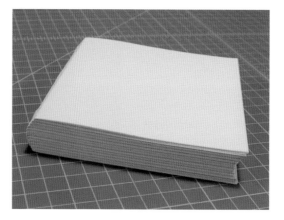

Fig. 5-41. Spine rounded to one-third of a circle

Step 4

Before attaching the endpapers to the front and back of the text block, fold the papers in half, with the "good side," or the sides that you want visible upon opening the book, folded inward. Use the bone folder to make a sharp crease along the fold (figs. 5-42 and 5-43).

The portion of the endpaper that gets tipped on to the text block is called the flyleaf. It becomes the first and last "leaves" of the text block. The endpaper portion that is glued to the front and back inside cover boards as you are attaching the text block to the case is called the pastedown.

Fig. 5-42. Fold endpapers with "good side" folded inward.

Fig. 5-43. Crease by using bone folder.

Step 5

To assist you in gluing the flyleaf, use a waste sheet that has been folded lengthwise to create a narrow, masked edge. Hold the folded waste sheet firmly in place on top of the flyleaf, with a second waste sheet underneath (fig. 5-44).

Fig. 5-44. Mask a narrow strip along endpaper fold with waste sheet.

It is important to place the folded waste sheet between ¹⁄₁₆" and no greater than ⅛" from the edge of the folded endpaper. Using PVA Thick, brush a narrow strip of glue along the folded edge of the endpaper (fig. 5-45).

Fig. 5-45. Hold mask firmly in place as you apply PVA Thick.

When gluing is completed, carefully remove the waste sheet to reveal a thin and neatly glued line of PVA Thick glue along the fold of the endpaper (fig. 5-46).

Fig. 5-46. Glue shown along folded edge of endpaper

Turn the glued flyleaf over and place it along the spine of the text block. The folded edge should be carefully lined up, parallel along the length of the spine edge and even with the head and tail of the text block. Press the endpaper down firmly, using the bone folder to ensure good contact (fig. 5-47).

Repeat this step on the other side of the text block to tip-in the second endpaper.

Fig. 5-47. Tip-in by aligning folded edge along fold of signature.

Step 6

Since the next several steps of the project require extensive handling of the text block, we recommend that you make a temporary protective case out of a heavier paper to help prevent damage. Basically, you want to cover the text block with a kraft paper or other heavier paper, leaving only the spine exposed.

For the size of the text pages in this project, we suggest you cut a piece of kraft paper measuring 7" × 15", with the grain running short. Center the text block with the exposed spine extending ⅛" over the long edge of the kraft paper. Fold the paper up and over the text block at the head and tail so that the pieces overlap at the center, and use masking tape to hold the case secure. Tuck in the two edges and bring the kraft paper over the fore-edge of the text block and secure with a second piece of masking tape. Except for the spine, the text block should now be completely covered and protected from further handling (fig. 5-48).

Fig. 5-48. Make a temporary protective case.

Step 7

To apply super (spine reinforcement) to the spine, loosely hold it lengthwise and pinch the super just at the head and tail to mark the midpoints. With scissors, snip a very small "V" shape at each crease, creating two notches to help identify the center along the length of the super (figs. 5-49 and 5-50).

Fig. 5-49. Snip a very small "V" shape at center of head and tail of super.

Fig. 5-50. Use "V" cuts to align super on spine of text block.

Before attaching the super, apply a light coat of PVA Thick to the spine. Use your finger to spread the glue between the two outside sewing stations along the spine (fig. 5-51).

Then, using the two sets of sewing stations as a reference, place the super on the spine so that it is centered and recessed evenly, ½" from both the head and tail. Approximately 1" of the super should overhang on both sides along the length of the spine, for later attachment to the cover boards.

Apply a second coat of PVA Thick to the spine, being careful not to use too much glue. Work the glue through the mesh until the super feels securely attached (fig. 5-52).

Fig. 5-51. Apply PVA Thick between two outside sewing stations.

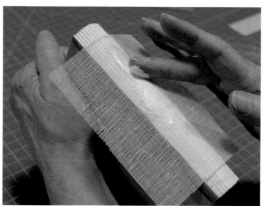

Fig. 5-52. Center super and apply second coat of PVA Thick.

Step 8

Accurately determine the spine width for cutting the spine lining, hollow tube, and spine inlay pieces. The best way to accurately measure the width of a rounded spine is to use a narrow strip of scrap paper about 1" wide and several times longer than the spine width. Wrap the paper tightly across the width of the spine and hold it firmly in place with your thumb and fingers.

Use your other hand to crease the paper strip at the two edges of the spine, and mark them with a pencil. Lay the paper strip on a ruler to measure the distance between the two marks, as accurately as possible to ⅟₃₂" (fig. 5-53).

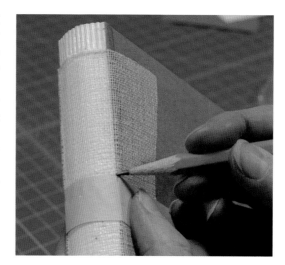

Fig. 5-53. Use strip of paper to accurately measure spine width.

Step 9

From this measurement, proceed to cut the spine lining, which is used to cover the super along the spine and to provide a smooth surface for gluing to the hollow-back tube.

The width is the width of the spine, as determined in the previous step, minus $\frac{1}{16}$", and the height is equal to the measurement between the two outside sewing stations. Almost any text paper will work for this purpose. The grain should run long. Using PVA, apply glue to the spine lining, and center carefully on the spine. Use your thumb first and then the bone folder to rub it down and make good contact (fig. 5-54).

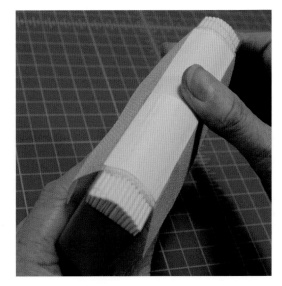

Fig. 5-54. Cut and glue spine-lining paper to spine.

Step 10

If you are attaching decorative headbands, you should have two equal pieces, both approximately 1¼" or slightly wider than the width of the spine. Before gluing the headbands in position, check that the fabric portion below the decorative bead will sit just above the sewing stations at the head and tail and not over them. Trim the fabric so that it sits just above the sewing, to reduce bulk along the spine.

Apply a small amount of PVA Thick across the spine, just slightly below the edge at the head and tail of the text block. Recessing the glue will allow for some oozing after the headbands are pressed into position (fig. 5-55).

Attach headbands both to the head and the tail of the spine, so that only the narrow decorative bead is visible above the text block and is facing the fore-edge of the book (fig. 5-56).

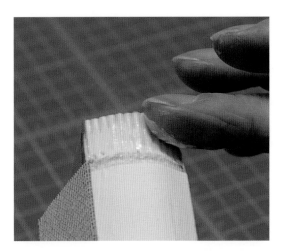

Fig. 5-55. Apply PVA Thick at head and tail across spine.

Fig. 5-56. Place headband bead facing toward fore-edge of text block.

After placing the headband in position, check to ensure that the decorative bead is parallel along the edge of the text block. If the headband is not aligned properly at this point, remove and reattach it. Otherwise, the unevenness will be noticeable after casing-in the text block (fig. 5-57).

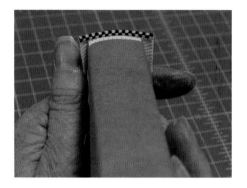

Fig. 5-57. Adjust headband bead so it is parallel across top of text block.

Fig. 5-58. Cut headbands flush with width of text block.

Fig. 5-59. Add dab of PVA Thick to headband bead to prevent unraveling.

Allow the headbands to dry for a few minutes. Then carefully trim each side with a sharp pair of scissors to the exact width of the spine (fig. 5-58).

To prevent the threads of the headband bead from unraveling, dab a very small amount of PVA Thick on the two cut edges of the headband bead (fig. 5-59).

Step 11

Create a hollow tube from kraft paper. The hollow tube serves two purposes. It is used to help push the text block away from the spine of the case when opened. It also provides for an easy method to attach the spine of the completed case to the rounded spine of the text block.

Using the spine measurement as determined in step 8, cut the hollow tube from kraft paper. The grain should run along the spine or in the long direction of the paper tube. The width of the kraft paper should be exactly three times the width of the spine, minus ¹⁄₁₆", or, in the case of the project, 2¹⁵⁄₁₆". The height of the hollow tube should be equal to the height of the text pages, or 5½", resulting in a cut dimension for the project of 2¹⁵⁄₁₆" × 5½".

Fig. 5-60a. Fold exactly one-third of width.

Carefully fold the kraft paper into three equal parts. Measure the width at exactly one-third and mark it in pencil. Make your first fold to that measurement and, using your bone folder, make a sharp crease along the fold line. To assist you, label this flap as "A." Bring the other side over flap "A" and line it up with the initial fold line. Firmly press down and crease with a bone folder to complete the trifold. This flap should be labeled "B" (figs. 5-60a and 5-60b).

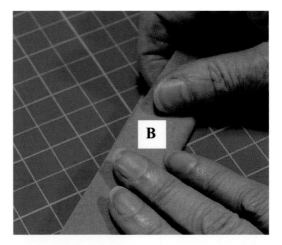

Fig. 5-60b. Complete by folding remainder over initial fold line.

Step 12

Before gluing the hollow tube to the spine, prime the attachment by first applying a light coat of PVA onto the spine-lining piece of the text block, as well as onto the headbands, just below the decorative bead. To glue the tube, position it with the two flaps facing down on a waste sheet, so that only the middle third of the trifold is visible. Apply a light coat of glue on this middle third of the hollow tube (fig. 5-61).

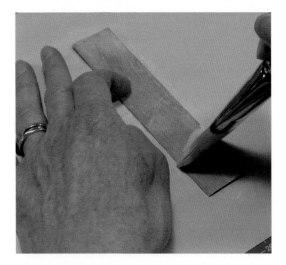

Fig. 5-61. Apply glue to middle third of hollow tube.

Attach the glued portion of the tube to the spine so that it is centered along the width of the spine and sits just between the decorative beads of the headbands. Press down lightly at first, check the positioning, and then firmly press into place to secure (fig. 5-62).

Fig. 5-62. Carefully position glued side of hollow tube onto spine.

Open the trifold and continue to press the glued portion down onto the spine. Use a bone folder to smooth out. At this point, it is especially important to ensure there is good contact between the spine and the headbands (fig. 5-63).

Refold the first flap ("A") over the spine and insert a small waste sheet underneath. Glue the top of the flap (fig. 5-64).

After removing the waste sheet, carefully bring the second flap ("B") on top of the glued flap ("A"). Press down to ensure good contact, and use the bone folder to apply additional pressure over the entire hollow tube to complete the attachment (fig. 5-65).

Fig. 5-63. Open folds and press down to ensure good contact.

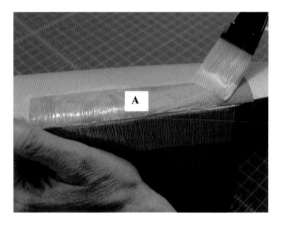

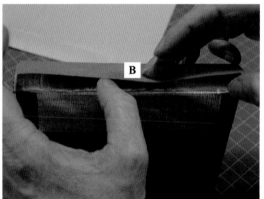

Fig. 5-64. Insert waste sheet under flap "A" and apply PVA.

Fig. 5-65. Bring flap "B" over top of "A" to create hollow tube.

Test the mechanics of the hollow tube by removing the protective kraft covering from the text block. Open the pages by grasping the first couple of signatures, with the spine facing upward. You should see the hollow tube pop open. Make sure no glue has seeped into the tube, causing it to stick together. In addition, look down the length of the tube to check whether it is glued securely along the length of the spine. If it is not, close the text block and continue to rub down along the spine (figs. 5-66 and 5-67).

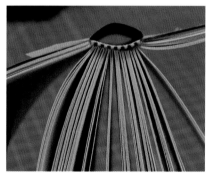

Fig. 5-66. Completed text block with protective case removed

Fig. 5-67. Test hollow tube for function.

PART IV.
CONSTRUCT THE CASE FOR THE TEXT BLOCK

Step 1

Cut the book board to the measurements as determined by the size of your text block, and on the basis of the project measurements. For the spine inlay, use the spine thickness of the text block as determined in part III, step 8. Then add 1/16" to the width to assist in creating the joint between the boards and the spine inlay.

Using the height of the book board and text block thickness for the project, the spine inlay measurement should be cut at 1 1/16" × 5¾", with grain long. Cut the spine inlay piece from a cover-weight paper or lightweight board such as card stock that is comparable to business card weight.

Step 2

Position the book cloth so that the side to be glued is facing up. Using a ruler or a spring divider, accurately find the midpoint across the width at the head and tail of the book cloth. Draw a pencil line running along the length at the center of the book cloth spine piece. In addition, mark the center of the spine inlay at the top and bottom with a pencil, to line up the spine piece with the center line on the book cloth (fig. 5-68).

Apply PVA to the spine inlay and place it on the book cloth, lining it up precisely with the two sets of lines. The spine inlay should also be centered so that there is an equal margin at the head and tail of the book cloth (fig. 5-69).

Fig. 5-68. Draw light pencil line accurately centered along length of book cloth.

Fig. 5-69. Add two centered marks to spine inlay and glue it to book cloth.

Step 3

Create a pair of ¼" spine-spacing guides (see the measuring guide instructions in chapter 2, "Fundamentals and Methods"). These spacing guides will help you quickly measure the ¼" gap between the spine board and the cover boards. This important gap produces the hinge or joint for the book covers. A ruler can also be used to measure the ¼" gap required for this purpose; however, spacing guides ensure that there is always an exact and consistent spacing.

Step 4

After the spine inlay has been attached, apply PVA to one side of the book cloth only. Be sure to hold the spine inlay firmly so the waste sheet does not shift as you are gluing, and remember to remove the waste sheet afterward. Place the two ¼" measuring guides directly against the edges of the spine inlay at the head and tail, with the ends of the guides resting off the book cloth for easy removal.

Place one of the cover boards against the two spacing guides. Make sure the cover board and spine inlay are aligned at the head and tail, then remove the guides. Once the guides are removed, the spine joint should be an even ¼" along the length of the spine (fig. 5-70).

Repeat this step, to attach the second cover board (fig. 5-71).

Fig. 5-70. Spacing guides create a ¼" joint.

Fig. 5-71. Use spacing guides again before attaching second cover board.

Step 5

Apply PVA to the book cloth at the head and tail, being careful not to overglue. Turn in the book cloth at both ends and press down onto the inside of the spine and cover boards. Be sure the book cloth is kept snug along the edges of the board as you turn in the cloth. Use the bone folder to assist you in pressing the book cloth into the gap between the spine and cover boards, to ensure there is good contact along the spine joints (fig. 5-72).

Turn the cover over and gently use your thumb along the spine gap to ensure that there is good contact on the outer side of the book cloth and to help define the outside and inside edges of the two joints (fig. 5-73).

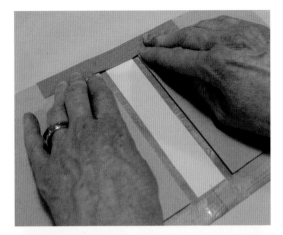

Fig. 5-72. Turn in book cloth at head and tail.

Fig. 5-73. Use thumb to form joint on outside of spine cloth.

Step 6

Before adding the trim strip, you may need to square the book cloth to the fore-edge of the covers. See chapter 2 if you need to trim the book cloth to an even margin. To place the trim strips before adding the decorative papers, use a ruler or divider to measure and mark the book cloth 3¼" from the fore-edge. The mark should be evident on both sides of the cover at the head and tail and should overlap the book cloth by ¼" (figs. 5-74 and 5-75).

Fig. 5-74. Measure from fore-edge to mark placement of trim strip.

Fig. 5-75. Use spring divider for quick and more-precise measurements.

It is helpful to place the case in a closed or angled position before applying the trim strip to the cover. Using the 3¼" marks, apply PVA to the trim strip and adhere it to the cover. When attaching the trim strip, line it up carefully so it is covering your two marks and remains parallel to the spine. Allow for an even ⅝" turn-in at the head and tail on the inside of the cover boards. Attach the trim strip on the other cover in the same manner (fig. 5-76).

Fig. 5-76. Attach decorative trim strip.

Step 7

To apply the decorative paper, measure 3" from the fore-edge. Mark on the trim strip at the head and tail and on both sides of the case. Glue the decorative paper over the trim strip so that it is aligned with and just covering the 3" marks. Ensure that the decorative paper is parallel to the trim strip and the spine. There should be an even ¼" margin of the trim strip evident. The three turn-ins at the head, tail, and fore-edge all should be approximately ⅝" (fig. 5-77).

Fig. 5-77. Attach decorative paper.

Step 8

After positioning the decorative paper, turn the cover over and miter the two outside corners, using scissors. The cuts should be at a 45° angle, leaving a space from the corner to the cut lines of approximately ⅛", or 1½ times the thickness of the book board (figs. 5-78 and 5-79).

Err on the side of having a little more margin rather than less when mitering the corner. A mitered cut at the corners that is cut twice the book board thickness is usually safer than one that is too tight. To assist you in getting this cut accurate, you can also use a ⅛" measuring guide.

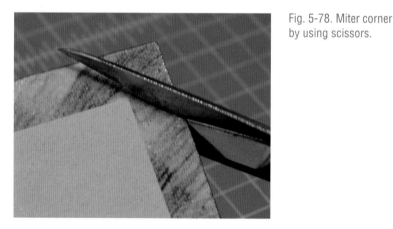

Fig. 5-78. Miter corner by using scissors.

Fig. 5-79. Corners mitered at 45° angle

Step 9

After both corners have been mitered, turn in the two short sides at the head and tail of the board and press down onto the inside of the cover. If at any point the glue appears to be drying after making the mitered cuts, lightly reglue the turn-ins (fig. 5-80).

At both mitered corners, make a slight tuck that is down and inward before turning in the fore-edge. When making the corner tucks, we will use our finger or a bone folder. This tuck is important for eliminating a small burr from protruding at the corners (fig. 5-81).

Fig. 5-80. Turn in two short sides onto inside cover.

Fig. 5-81. Tuck in corners by using bone folder.

Step 10

Bring the long turn-in over the fore-edge of the board and press down onto the inside of the cover. Smooth the corners by tapping them or applying gentle pressure with the bone folder (figs. 5-82 and 5-83).

Fig. 5-82. Turn in fore-edge onto inside cover.

Fig. 5-83. Tap corners to gently round them.

Step 11

Repeat steps 6 through 10 on the other cover to complete the attachment of the decorative trim strips and papers (fig. 5-84).

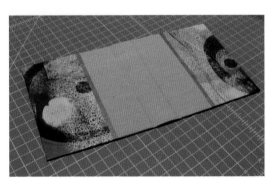

Fig. 5-84. Completed book cover with trim strips

PART V.
CASE-IN THE TEXT BLOCK

Step 1

Visually check the text block in the case, without gluing. Lay the case open and flat. Holding the text block upright, set the spine of the text block on the spine inlay and press down firmly. The spine will temporarily flatten during this part of the step.

Align the edges of the spine of the text block with the edges of the spine inlay, so that you see a slight margin along both sides of the spine inlay. In addition, visually check the margin of the headbands, which should be evenly recessed at the head and tail of the spine (fig. 5-85).

Next, close the covers over the text block so that the hollow back is pressed firmly against the spine of the case. While holding the book upright, re-create the rounded spine by applying pressure along the fore-edge, toward the spine. At the same time, use your other hand to push the covers toward the fore-edge. The margins at the fore-edge, head, and tail should be square and extend approximately ⅛" (fig. 5-86).

Fig. 5-85. Check fit of text block along spine and headbands before gluing.

Fig. 5-86. Re-create the round by applying equal pressure at fore-edge and spine.

Step 2

To help secure the attachment of the hollow tube of the text block to the case, apply a light coat of PVA to the spine inlay and into the joints. Include gluing up to ¼" onto the book cloth turn-ins at the head and tail. Avoid over-gluing, especially in the joints, to help prevent excess glue from seeping out when the book is pressed (fig. 5-87).

Fig. 5-87. Apply PVA to spine inlay and into joints of case.

Step 3

Pick up the text block and apply PVA to the entire hollow tube along the spine. Again, it is important not to overglue, especially near the two openings of the hollow tube, to prevent it from being glued shut (fig. 5-88).

As was determined in step 1, carefully center the hollow tube on the spine inlay. Apply enough pressure so that you compress the spine of the text block. It should lie flat and make firm contact with the spine inlay (fig. 5-89). Then, as shown in step 1, close the covers and apply pressure along the fore-edge, toward the spine, while applying an equal pressure along the edges of the book board covers toward the fore-edge. This will help reshape the spine.

Using your thumb, press down on the book cloth along the entire spine of the case. Apply enough pressure to help ensure that there is solid contact between the spine inlay and the hollow tube, as well as the headbands (fig. 5-90).

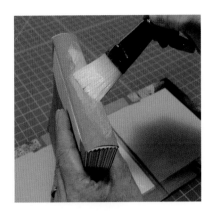

Fig. 5-88. Apply PVA carefully to hollow-back tube.

Fig. 5-89. Center text block onto spine inlay.

Fig. 5-90. Press down along outside of spine.

Step 4

Use the bone folder along the joint to define and tighten the hinge on both sides of the spine. The pressure applied with the bone folder should be firm, but avoid using too much pressure with the pointed end, since it may tear through the book cloth. This step helps define the joint between the spine inlay and the edges of the cover boards (fig. 5-91).

Fig. 5-91. Define joint between spine inlay and cover boards.

Step 5

Position the book so that the fore-edge of the text block is facing you, and one of the covers is leaning against a support object. Insert a waste sheet between the flyleaf and pastedown and place it so that it fits snugly against the inside fold (fig. 5-92).

Fig. 5-92. Insert waste sheet between flyleaf and pastedown.

Lift the super just enough so that you can apply a coat of PVA under the spine reinforcement material and onto the pastedown (fig. 5-93).

Fig. 5-93. Brush glue onto pastedown underneath super.

After this initial coat of glue is applied, use your brush to press the super down onto the pastedown. Apply a thin coat of glue on top of the super and continue to glue the entire pastedown (fig. 5-94).

Be careful not to apply too much glue at the head and tail near the spine. This will help avoid glue from seeping out once the book is cased-in and placed under weights or in a book press. Carefully remove the waste sheet when gluing is completed.

Fig. 5-94. Press down super and continue to glue entire pastedown.

Step 6

With the traditional method of casing-in, at this point you would simply close the covers onto the glued pastedown. This process sometimes leaves the pastedowns out of square. We offer an alternative to this method that helps ensure the pastedowns are glued square to the covers.

To accomplish a square pastedown, lift up the two outside corners and place them on the inside book cover, so that the same visual margin of ⅛" corresponds to what was evident in step 1. Once this alignment occurs, press only the top half of the pastedown onto the board, while keeping the cover in an upright position (fig. 5-95).

Rotate the book 180° so that the book cover is now flat on the table and facing toward you. At the same time, grasp the text block and the back cover and hold it upright. With your one hand in this position, use your other hand to press down the bottom portion of the pastedown, working it slowly toward the spine (fig. 5-96).

Avoid using a bone folder at the spine, to prevent accidentally tearing the pastedown at the hinge. Using firm finger pressure is enough to help secure the pastedown to the inside cover.

Fig. 5-95. Attach top half of pastedown to cover.

Fig. 5-96. Rotate book and press down bottom half of pastedown.

Step 7

Place a piece of wax paper, cut slightly larger than the length and width of the text block, between the glued pastedown and the flyleaf. The wax paper will prevent moisture from the glue from being absorbed by the flyleaf and first few pages of the text block, which would cause buckling. The wax paper also ensures that any glue that might seep out as the book is pressed does not damage the text block (fig. 5-97).

Fig. 5-97. Insert wax paper between pastedown and flyleaf.

Step 8

Repeat steps 5 through 7 and glue the second pastedown. Allow for a square ⅛" margin at the fore-edge and along the head and tail, as with the first cover.

As you glue the second pastedown, you may need to hold the cover at a lower angle to accurately position the pastedown, because the other side has already been glued to the first cover board and there is less play along the spine.

After turning the book cover 180°, as shown in step 6, grasp the cover board along with the text block and keep it at a slightly lower angle as you press the pastedown toward the spine. Since there is less play along the spine, this will help reduce the tension as the second pastedown is attached.

Add a second piece of wax paper between the pastedown and flyleaf when completed.

Step 9

With the book now closed, use the bone folder to apply even and firm pressure along the two joints between the board covers and the spine on both sides of the case (fig. 5-98).

Firm pressure applied by the bone folder in the joint will help ensure tighter contact of the text block to the book cover. This will also define the joint to place the joint rods. A joint wire rod thickness of 1⁄16" (2 mm) is ideal. We use the long, straight bottom portion of a wire clothes hanger as rods. A pair of thin knitting needles (size 0) are also a good size for this purpose (fig. 5-99). Although it is not essential to add the wire rods, we have found that it helps define and tighten the joint, giving the book a cleaner look when completed.

Fig. 5-98. Apply firm pressure along joint, using bone folder.

Fig. 5-99. Add joint rods along hinge.

Step 10

Set your completed book between two pressing boards, with a clean waste sheet in between the boards and your book. Be careful to ensure that the wire rods are kept securely in the joints during this process (fig. 5-100).

Place a couple of heavy weights (5 to 10 lbs.) on top of the pressing boards and allow your book to dry overnight with the wax paper remaining in place. A book press can also be used, but we advise against using too much pressure, which can cause glue to ooze along the spine.

Fig. 5-100. Set book between press boards and add heavy weights.

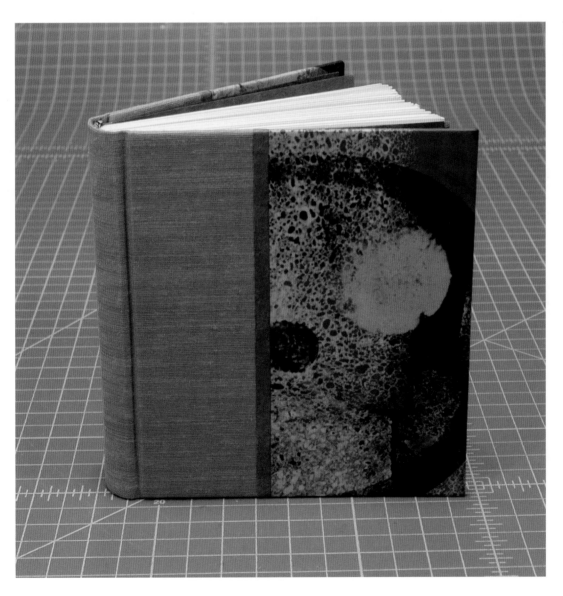

The completed Round-Back Book Project

The Slipcase

The slipcase is an open-edge box that is constructed slightly larger than the book that it is designed to hold. Although it is not intended to be as protective as a clamshell box, it is easier to construct and serves the purpose of storing and preventing damage to the book covers and text block. The method presented in this chapter produces a traditional slipcase style, constructed and covered using basic box making techniques.

There are many variations of how to make a slipcase. Some are made from thin cardboard and simply scored and folded. More-complex slipcases include double-thick walls, notches along the side panels, and curved fore-edges to correspond to the shape of a rounded spine. The focus of this chapter is to make a slipcase for the flat-back book project.

The most important consideration in making a slipcase is accuracy in measuring the board pieces. A slipcase should be constructed so the book fits comfortably, with care taken that it is neither too loose nor too tight. In this chapter we present a method that allows you to determine the appropriate measurements for a slipcase, on the basis of the dimensions of your book, with very little margin for error. For this project we used .090 / 3/32" book board, which matches the thickness used for the flat-back project.

Slipcase project with flat-back book

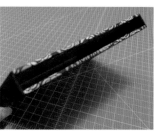

Lining paper matches flyleaf of flat-back book.

MATERIALS, TOOLS, AND SUPPLIES

PROJECT MATERIALS, DIMENSIONS, GRAIN DIRECTION, AND QUANTITIES

Materials

Book board (.090 or ³⁄₃₂" thickness)
Book cloth
Decorative paper
Lining paper
PVA
PVA Thick

Tools

Bone folder
C-clamp
Cutting knives
Cutting mat
Glue brushes
Makeshift tools (glue applicator, scraper, measuring guides)
Press boards
Ruler
Scissors
Spring divider
Square
Support board
Weights

Supplies

Damp cloth
Masking tape
Paper towels
Pencil
Sandpaper
Sponge
Waste sheets
Wax paper

The following measurements were determined on the basis of the exact dimensions of the flat-back project and are listed only as a reference. Your measurements may differ from ours. For this project you will need to determine your own measurements, on the basis of the size of your book. Formulas for cutting all your materials for this structure are listed in chapter 8, "Book and Box Making Formulas."

Materials	Dimensions	Grain Direction	Quantity
Book Board			
Front and Back Panels	5⅞" × 7½"	Long	(2)
Head and Tail Walls	⅝" × 5¾" (+)	Long	(2)
Spine Wall	⅝" × 7½"	Long	(1)
Lining Paper for Book Board			
Front and Back Lining	7" × 8½"	Long	(2)
Head and Tail Lining	1⅝" × 6¾"	Long	(2)
Spine Lining	1⅝" × 8½"	Long	(1)
Book Cloth			
Head and Tail Book Cloth	1⅞" × 6¼"	Long	(2)
Spine Book Cloth	1⅞" × 8¾"	Long	(1)
Decorative Paper			
Front and Back Paper	6⅜" × 7¼"	Long	(2)

PART I.
CALCULATE THE HEIGHT, WIDTH, AND THICKNESS OF THE BOOK

Before cutting the board pieces for the slipcase project, you will need to determine the measurements of your book. Begin by measuring the width, height, and spine thickness of the completed book after it has been dried and pressed under weights. These measurements should be as precise as possible.

Step 1

To determine the width of your book, measure from the spine to the fore-edge. Place a square flush against the spine and measure with a ruler. Record the width, rounding up to the nearest ⅟₃₂" (fig. 6-1).

Fig. 6-1. Use a square and ruler to measure width of book.

Measure the height of the book in the same manner, but with the square flush against the head or tail. Record the height, rounding up to the nearest ⅟₃₂" (fig. 6-2).

 Measure each of these dimensions at several points along the width and height, and use the largest measurement.

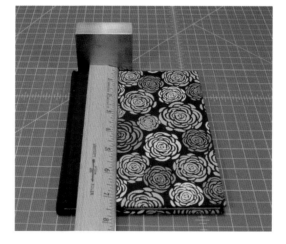

Fig. 6-2. Use a square and ruler to measure height of book.

Step 2

To determine the thickness of the book there are two methods you can use. In the first method, place a piece of square book board with the edge set against the spine of the book. Next, place a thin metal straightedge across the cover along the width of the book and mark the edge of the book board where it meets the straightedge using a sharpened pencil. In the same manner, check a couple of additional measurements along the head or tail of the book to assure the thickness is consistent. Measure the distance marked on the square book board and record the spine thickness (fig. 6-3).

Fig. 6-3. Use a book board square and straightedge to measure thickness.

The second method is to use a spring divider to measure the spine thickness. Close the divider so the inside points are just touching the outer edges along the spine. You will then need to transfer this distance to a ruler and record the measurement. Since sometimes the thickness of the book is greatest along the head or tail of the book, be sure to measure the book's thickness at several points along the width, and again, use the largest measurement (fig. 6-4).

Fig. 6-4. Use a spring divider to measure thickness of book.

Step 3

Record these three measurements:

Width _____ × Height _____ × Spine thickness _____
Example: 5¾" × 7¼" × 9⁄16"

PART II.
CUT BOOK BOARD AND
ATTACH LINING PIECES

Step 1

Cut the book board pieces, using the measurements as determined by the size of your book and using the formulas in chapter 8. Be sure to check all measurements carefully and round up to the nearest $\frac{1}{32}$" for all five board pieces. This will ensure the best fit of the book when the slipcase is completed.

The lining pieces will be trimmed, so accuracy is not as important. They can be rounded up or down to the nearest $\frac{1}{8}$" (fig. 6-5).

Fig. 6-5. Book board and lining pieces

Step 2

After board pieces have been cut, we recommend that you double check three measurements for accuracy before proceeding. Place your completed book on one of the two book board side panels so that it is flush with the tail and spine of the book. Use a solid support to ensure that the two pieces are flush (fig. 6-6).

Measure the margin between the head of the book and the head of the side panel board. This measurement should be $\frac{1}{4}$". Use a ruler or measuring guide to ensure accuracy. (See chapter 2, "Fundamentals and Methods," for making measuring guides.)

Next check the margin at the fore-edge of the book. The margin between the fore-edge of the book and fore-edge of the side panel should be $\frac{1}{8}$" (fig. 6-7).

Fig. 6-6. Use squares to align book at spine and tail on side-panel book board.

Fig. 6-7. Check height and width margins with measuring guides.

Finally, check the accuracy of the spine thickness. Place the spine board edge so it is sitting on top of the side panel and flush against the spine of the book. There should be a space of 1/16" between the top edge of the spine board and the cover of the book. Use a 1/16" measuring guide to check the accuracy by laying the measuring guide on the spine of the book and against the spine board. The top edge of the spine board should be flush with the measuring guide (fig. 6-8).

Fig. 6-8. Check accuracy of spine thickness.

Step 3

After cutting the book board pieces for the slipcase and checking for accuracy, you will need to glue the lining paper to prevent the board from warping after the outside of the slipcase is covered. Before gluing the lining papers, we suggest you dampen the paper on the opposite side of the "good" side, especially when using a commercial paper. After the paper begins to absorb the moisture, it will start to curl. Within a few seconds, the paper will relax. This process will help prevent the paper from wrinkling when glued to the book board.

Spread a thin coat of PVA on the book board and not on the paper (fig. 6-9).

After the entire piece is glued, turn the board over and place it on to the dampened side of the lining paper. Center the board so there is approximately an equal 1/2" margin of paper on all four sides (fig. 6-10).

Fig. 6-9. Glue one side of panel book board.

Fig. 6-10. Place board on side opposite "good" side.

Turn the board over and smooth the paper by using finger pressure. If you are using a bone folder, first place a waste sheet over the paper before rubbing down. Be sure to press down firmly along the outer edges to make good contact with the board. Attach all five board pieces to the lining papers in this same manner (fig. 6-11).

Fig. 6-11. Press along four edges.

After the pieces are glued, allow them to dry for about five to ten minutes before trimming them. Place a small weight on the boards to prevent them from warping as they begin to dry. If the boards do start to warp, gently bend them the opposite way so that they will lie flat before you proceed (fig. 6-12).

Fig. 6-12. Weight board pieces while drying.

Step 4

Turn the boards over so the linings are face down on your cutting mat. Using a light-duty cutting knife, carefully trim all the edges of the lining papers so that they are cut flush to the board (fig. 6-13).

Make sure you use a new blade during this step to achieve clean cuts. Set the blade firmly against the edge of the book board and use it as a guide for trimming. When completed, the five boards with linings will be ready for constructing the slipcase (fig. 6-14).

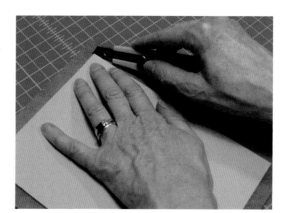

Fig. 6-13. Trim linings against edge of boards.

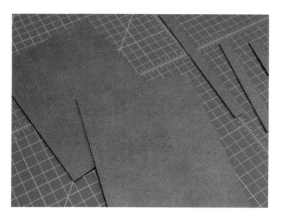

Fig. 6-14. Board pieces with linings trimmed

PART III.
CONSTRUCT THE SLIPCASE

Step 1

For constructing the slipcase, it is helpful to use a support board or some other means to brace the walls of the slipcase. We use a ¾" wood board, cut to approximately 3" × 12", but anything similar will work. You will need at least one clamp to hold the board securely in place. To prevent glue from sticking to the board, you can wrap wax paper around one long edge of support board. Set the long edge of one of the side panels in front of you, with the lining side up and so the book board is braced against the front edge of the support (fig. 6-15).

Fig. 6-15. Place long edge of side panel against support.

Step 2

For gluing the slipcase board pieces together, you will need to use PVA Thick as well as a thick-glue applicator and a scraper tool (see chapter 2 on how to fabricate these two simple makeshift tools).

Using the applicator, apply a small amount of thick glue to only one of the long edges of the spine board wall. Use a dabbing motion when applying the glue, rather than attempting to brush it on. This will help obtain a uniform "bead" of glue along the entire edge of the book board. Be careful not to overglue. You want to apply just enough thick glue for the board edges to make solid contact, with minimal need for scraping off excess glue (fig. 6-16).

Fig. 6-16. Glue one long edge of spine wall.

Step 3

After gluing the long edge of the spine wall, place it on top of the panel with the lining side inward, forming a 90° angle. The spine board should be even with the panel edge and flush with the two side edges of the panel (fig. 6-17).

Apply an equal amount of pressure, both downward and against the support board, and hold in place for several seconds so that it maintains that position. Scrape off any excess glue with the scraper tool, then carefully move the two glued pieces away from the support board.

Fig. 6-17. Place spine wall on side panel against support board.

Step 4

Rotate the side panel so that either the head or tail edge of the panel is now braced against the support (fig. 6-18).

Without gluing, hold the head or tail piece to be glued in place against the support board to determine which long and short side will need to be glued (fig. 6-19).

Fig. 6-18. Rotate side panel so that spine wall is perpendicular to support board.

Fig. 6-19. Determine orientation of head or tail wall before gluing.

Consider that the lining side will be facing inward, and the short side will butt up to the spine wall. Proceed to apply PVA Thick to the appropriate short edge and long edge of the head or tail wall (figs. 6-20 and 6-21).

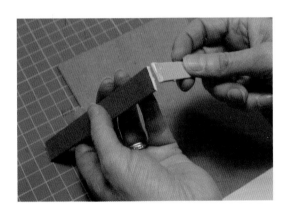

Fig. 6-20. Glue only one short edge of head or tail wall.

Fig. 6-21. Glue only one long edge of same piece.

Step 5

After the head or tail piece is glued on the two edges, position it on the side panel against the support board so that the lining side is facing inward and the glued short edge butts up against the spine wall (fig. 6-22).

Apply firm pressure along the glued edges and hold in place at a 90° angle against the support for several seconds. Carefully move the slipcase away from the support board and rotate the structure to glue the opposite short wall in the same manner.

Adjust the three side walls relative to the side panel. The head, tail, and spine pieces should be positioned at a 90° angle, and all the edges flush with the edges of the side panel. If needed, use a scraper to remove any excess glue from inside the slipcase along the glued edges (fig. 6-23).

Allow some time for the glue to dry along the edges, and then check the fit of the book one last time in the partially constructed slipcase. The spacing between the book's head and tail and the two short walls should be in the range of ⅟₃₂" on either side, or ⅟₁₆" total. The book should be recessed from the top edge of the spine board ⅟₁₆", as shown in fig. 6-8. The book should also be recessed ⅟₃₂" from the open end of the tray (fig. 6-24).

Step 6

Attach the second side panel by applying a thin bead of PVA Thick along the top three edges of the slipcase walls (fig. 6-25).

Fig. 6-22. Place short wall so it butts up to spine wall.

Fig. 6-23. Adjust edges of three walls.

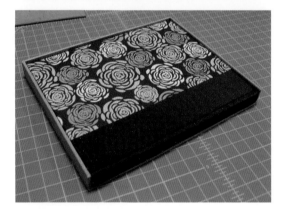

Fig. 6-24. Check fit of book in tray before proceeding.

Fig. 6-25. Glue top edges of the three walls.

Make sure the panel lining faces the inside of the slipcase. This second panel should sit evenly with the top edges of the three side walls (fig. 6-26).

Fig. 6-26. Set second panel onto glued edges.

Press the panel down firmly and adjust the boards so that all the edges are flush. If it is difficult to adjust the inside back portion of the slipcase, use a long, sturdy implement such as a ruler or long glue brush handle. This will enable you to exert enough pressure to assist in nudging the side panels or narrow walls as needed to even the edges (figs. 6-27 and 6-28).

Fig. 6-27. Apply firm pressure along edges.

Fig. 6-28. Adjust back edges of slipcase if necessary.

Because it may be difficult to remove excess glue inside the slipcase after setting the panel in place, beware of overgluing. If a little extra glue remains inside the slipcase, it is not a problem. However, a long makeshift scraper tool can remove most of the excess glue (fig. 6-29).

Fig. 6-29. Remove excess glue with long glue scraper.

In addition, if the side panels tend to pull away from the walls, a few small pieces of masking tape can be used to hold them together. After the glue dries, the tape can be removed (fig. 6-30).

Fig. 6-30. Use masking tape to hold panels in place if needed.

Step 7

Check the slipcase for squareness by placing it on a flat surface upright on the head or tail with a steel square against each side panel. Turn it over and check other side. Accurately measuring, cutting, and constructing the slipcase should keep it square. However, if either side is slightly out of square, you may need to carefully use a light-duty knife to cut the pieces apart where they were glued, re-glue, and adjust the sides before proceeding. Allow the slipcase to dry for about ten minutes. If there is a slight unevenness, use a fine or medium grit sandpaper to smooth out uneven edges (fig. 6-31).

Fig. 6-31. Use sandpaper to smooth rough edges.

PART IV.
COVER THE SLIPCASE

There are a variety of ways to cover a slipcase. We prefer a five-piece covering method, which is both elegant and easy to learn. The five pieces include three pieces of book cloth for the outside walls and two decorative papers for the side panels (fig. 6-32).

Fig. 6-32. Cover materials for slipcase.

Step 1

After cutting the cover pieces, begin by applying PVA to the spine book cloth piece (fig. 6-33).

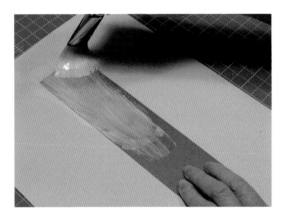

Fig. 6-33. Apply PVA to book cloth spine.

Center the spine of the slipcase on the book cloth, making sure that there is a margin of approximately ⅝" for the turn-ins at the head and tail and along the side panels (fig. 6-34).

Fig. 6-34. Center slipcase spine on book cloth.

Step 2

Press down along the spine first and then bring the two turn-ins onto the side panels (fig. 6-35).

Fig. 6-35. Turn in book cloth onto side panels.

At the four corners of the spine, the book cloth will form 90° angles. Help define these four angles by creasing or pinching the corners with your thumb and forefinger (fig. 6-36).

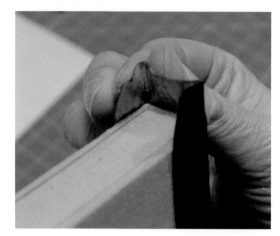

Fig. 6-36. Form 90° angles at each of four corners.

Step 3

Hold the slipcase upright so that you are viewing one of the corners. Carefully bring the scissors in from the outside corner, mitering a small triangle that will form a narrow "V" shape in the book cloth. It is important to elevate the scissors slightly when beginning the miter, to ensure you don't cut into the corner edges of the book board (fig. 6-37).

Fig. 6-37. Miter a "V" shape at each corner.

Repeat this step at the other three corners, resulting in two sets of three small tabs at the head and tail of the slipcase (fig. 6-38).

Fig. 6-38. Two "V" cuts create three small tabs.

Step 4

At one end of the slipcase, turn in the two small side tabs onto the head or tail wall. Next, turn in the single middle tab onto the head or tail wall, covering the two side tabs (fig. 6-39).

Fig. 6-39. Turn in two side tabs onto head and tail.

Repeat this process at the other end of the slipcase to completely cover the two corners at the head and tail. Use the bone folder to tap or press the corners and remove any burrs that might form (fig. 6-40).

Fig. 6-40. Turn in middle tab to cover two side tabs.

Step 5

Glue the book cloth piece used for the head or tail. Place the head or tail of the slipcase on the book cloth, with the short edge of the book cloth spine recessed ⅛" from the spine edge of the slipcase (figs. 6-41 and 6-42).

Fig. 6-41. Center slipcase head or tail on book cloth.

Fig. 6-42. Close-up of ⅛" recess at spine edge

At the same time, allow for an equal ⅝" turn-in onto the side panels and a ⅝" turn-in at the open end of the slipcase. Bring the turn-ins over the short edges of the panels and press down onto the boards (fig. 6-43).

Fig. 6-43. Turn in head or tail piece onto side panels.

Step 6

At the two front corners or open ends of the slipcase, the turn-ins will form 90° angles. Help define the angles by creasing or pinching the two corners with your thumb and forefinger, as in step 2 (fig. 6-44).

Fig. 6-44. Form 90° angle corners at open end of slipcase.

Rotate the slipcase so that you are now looking into it at the open end. From this position, make a pair of straight cuts toward the front edge of the board. These two cuts should be made so the blade of the scissors is cutting on a line that is flush with the inside wall of the side panels (fig. 6-45).

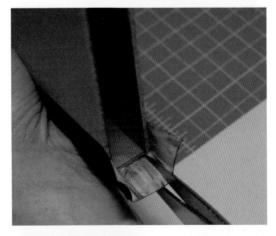

Fig. 6-45. Two straight cuts at open end, flush with inside walls

The result of the two cuts will be three narrow tabs at the open end (fig. 6-46).

Fig. 6-46. Three tabs formed after two straight cuts

Step 7

The center tab is cut so it is recessed ⅛" from the outside of the side panels, which is slightly more than the thickness of the book board. Press in the two outside tabs, which will start to wrap or twist around the inside corner (fig. 6-47).

After the side tabs are pressed into the corners, turn in the center tab, which will now fit precisely between the two side panels (figs. 6-48 and 6-49).

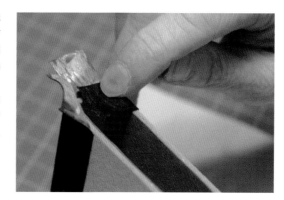

Fig. 6-47. Turn in two outside tabs to wrap around inside corners.

Fig. 6-48. Tabs turned in and covering two inside corners

Fig. 6-49. Press down center tab between side panels.

Step 8

Use the bone folder to help work the tabs into the two inner corners. The bone folder should also be used to compress and shape the outside corners. When this step is completed, the two side tabs will be covered and help reinforce the four corners of the slipcase (figs. 6-50 and 6-51).

Fig. 6-50. Use bone folder to press center tab into corners.

Fig. 6-51. Press outside corners with bone folder to flatten and shape.

Step 9

Place the decorative paper on the panel to check the margins before gluing. The decorative paper should be recessed ⅛" from the outside spine edge. In addition, the side panel should be placed so that it is recessed an equal ⅛" from the head and tail of the slipcase, creating a square margin of ⅛" at the three edges. At the open edge the decorative-paper turn-in should extend ⅝" to match the book cloth turn-ins (fig. 6-52).

If you are using a commercial paper, your paper may stretch after glue is applied. This may affect the ⅝" turn-in at the fore-edge of the slipcase. You may want to wet your paper and remeasure the turn-in before gluing. See chapter 2 regarding paper stretch.

Step 10

Glue and carefully center the decorative paper on the panel, as previewed in the previous step. Alignment is important, since placing the paper even at a slight angle at the spine edge can lead to it being out of position at the fore-edge. Bring the decorative-paper turn-in over the edge and press down along the inside of the slipcase (figs. 6-53 and 6-54).

Fig. 6-52. Align side-panel decorative paper.

Fig. 6-53. Decorative-paper alignment before turn-in

Fig. 6-54. Turn in fore-edge onto inside panel.

The correct alignment will allow the turn-ins to fit neatly just to the inside of the head and tail walls. Each decorative-paper turn-in should line up evenly with the book cloth turn-ins on the inside of the slipcase (fig. 6-55).

Repeat this step with the other decorative paper.

Step 11

Before the slipcase is put under weights to dry, the book should be inserted for support. Use wax paper to protect the book against glue and dampness from the slipcase. The wax paper should be cut so that it is the same height as the book.

Wrap the wax paper around the fore-edge, leaving the spine edge of the book open before inserting it into the slipcase (figs. 6-56 and 6-57).

Fig. 6-55. All turn-ins aligned evenly on inside of slipcase

Fig. 6-56. Wrap fore-edge of flat-back book with wax paper.

Fig. 6-57. Place book inside slipcase.

Step 12

With the book inside the slipcase and still wrapped with wax paper, place them between two press boards (fig. 6-58).

Fig. 6-58. Book in slipcase between two press boards

Add weights (2 to 3 pounds) on top and allow the slipcase to dry overnight (fig. 6-59).

Fig. 6-59. Weight and allow to dry overnight.

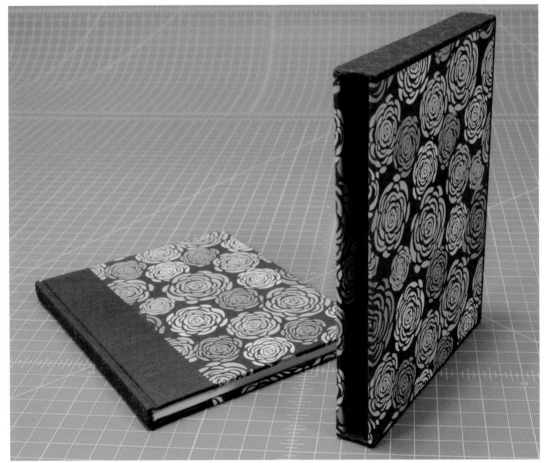

The completed Slipcase Project

The Clamshell Box

The clamshell box is considered one of the sturdiest and most protective box structures. Although it is primarily used for books, it can also be used to hold art prints, documents, loose papers, and other items. It is sometimes referred to as a two-tray drop-spine box. As the name implies, the box is composed of two trays with a spine that lies flat when the box is open, allowing for easy removal of the book.

There are various ways to construct a clamshell box. The method presented in this chapter is a common style for most sizes, although oversized or very heavy books might benefit by using thicker book board and reinforced corners. Some clamshell boxes include built-in slipcases, drop fronts, removable trays, and even secret compartments.

An important consideration in constructing a clamshell box is accuracy in measuring the board pieces. The book should fit comfortably inside the small tray, with the large tray being just slightly larger. Formulas for cutting all your materials for this structure are included in chapter 8, "Book and Box Making Formulas." For this project we used .090 / ³⁄₃₂" book board, matching the thickness used for the round-back project.

Completed clamshell box with round-back book

MATERIALS, TOOLS, AND SUPPLIES

Materials

Book board (.090 or 3/32" thickness)
Book cloth
Decorative paper
PVA
PVA Thick

Tools

Bone folder
Cutting knives
Cutting mat
Glue brushes
Makeshift tools (glue applicator, scraper, measuring guides)
Press boards
Ruler
Scissors
Spring divider
Square
Weights

Supplies

Damp cloth
Masking tape
Paper towels
Pencil
Sandpaper (fine to medium grit)
Sponge
Waste sheets
Wax paper

PROJECT MATERIALS, DIMENSIONS, GRAIN DIRECTION, AND QUANTITIES

The following measurements were determined on the basis of the exact dimensions of the round-back project and are listed only as a reference. Your measurements may differ from ours. For this project you will need to determine your own measurements based on the size of your book.

Materials	*Dimensions*	*Grain Direction*	*Quantity*
Book Board			
Lid	6" × 6¾"	Long	(2)
Spine	1 9/16" × 6¾"	Long	(1)
Small Tray Bottom	5½" × 5⅞"	Long	(1)
Long Wall	1 5/16" × 6 1/16"	Long	(1)
Short Walls	1 5/16" × 5½"	Long	(2)
Large Tray Bottom	5 11/16" × 6 3/16"	Long	(1)
Long Wall	1½" × 6⅜"	Long	(1)
Short Walls	1½" × 5 11/16"	Long	(2)
Decorative Paper			
Lid	4½" × 8¼"	Long	(2)
Trim Strip	¾" × 8¼"	Long	(2)
Small Tray Bottom	6¼" × 5¾"	Long	(1)
Long Wall	3⅝" × 7⅛"	Long	(1)
Short Walls	3⅝" × 6"	Long	(2)
Large Tray Bottom	6½" × 6 1/16"	Long	(1)
Long Wall	3⅞" × 7⅜"	Long	(1)
Short Walls	3⅞" × 6¼"	Long	(2)
Book Cloth			
Outside Spine	6⅞" × 8¼"	Long	(1)
Inside Spine	3⅝" × 5 15/16"	Long	(1)

PART I.
CONSTRUCT THE TRAYS

Step 1

After measuring and cutting all the book board pieces, organize them into three sets. It is helpful to label each piece for easy identification. You will need wax paper, PVA Thick, a thick glue applicator, and a scraper tool to construct the trays (fig. 7-1).

1. Lid: top and bottom lid and spine—three pieces
2. Large tray: bottom, long wall, and two short walls—four pieces
3. Small tray: bottom, long wall, and two short walls—four pieces

Fig. 7-1. Materials for lid and trays

Step 2

Cut a piece of wax paper several inches larger than the size of the small tray bottom and tape it down on your work surface. The wax paper will allow for an easier release of the pieces after they have been glued. Use a short edge of the glue applicator to apply PVA Thick to one of the two long edges of the tray bottom piece. Try to obtain a uniform "bead" of glue along the edge without overgluing (fig. 7-2).

Rotate the tray bottom so that you can apply a bead of glue along the two short edges. Once you have completed gluing these three edges, set it down on the wax paper.

Fig. 7-2. Glue one long edge and two short edges of small tray bottom.

Step 3

Apply thick glue to only ONE short edge of the short walls of the small tray (fig. 7-3).

Fig. 7-3. Glue along one short edge of small-tray short walls.

Next, attach the short wall to the small tray bottom by pressing the edges of the short walls to the glued short edges of the tray bottom (fig. 7-4).

Both short walls should be flush with the short edge of the tray bottom, so that all three glued edges are oriented at the same end of the tray. Push firmly against the short edge pieces of the tray bottom to ensure good contact, so that they are positioned at a 90° angle.

Fig. 7-4. Attach short walls to small tray bottom, with three glued edges in alignment.

Step 4

There is no need to apply thick glue to the long wall. Simply position the long wall so that it is aligned evenly with the previously glued two short edges and the bottom edge of the tray (fig 7-5).

Push firmly along the long edge so that a small amount of glue oozes out. Take several moments to adjust all the walls and maintain a 90° angle. Scrape off any excess glue from inside the tray, using the makeshift scraper. In addition, brush off any dried glue on the inside or outside of the tray so that all the surfaces are clean and smooth (fig. 7-6).

Fig. 7-5. Position long wall against bottom edge of tray and two short walls.

Fig. 7-6. Remove excess glue.

Step 5

Complete the large tray by repeating steps 2 through 4.

Accurately measuring, cutting, and constructing your trays will reduce the unevenness when the trays are glued together. However, use a fine- or medium-grit sandpaper to smooth out any rough edges if needed.

Step 6

Check the fit of the two trays by first setting the small tray tight into the corner of the large tray. There should be between ¹⁄₁₆" and ⅛" space between the two trays along the head and tail. At the fore-edge, or open end of the two nesting trays, there should be a margin of ¹⁄₁₆". In addition, there should be ¹⁄₃₂" difference in the wall height between the small tray and the large tray. Use the measuring guides suggested in chapter 2, "Fundamentals and Methods," to assist in checking these measurements (fig. 7-7).

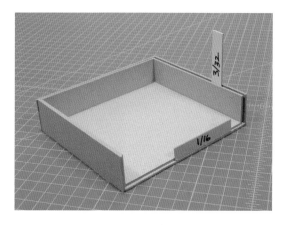

Fig. 7-7. Check fit of small tray in large tray.

Next, set the completed round-back book in the small tray to check the fit of the book. The margin between the head or tail of the small tray walls should be ¹⁄₁₆". The margin from the spine to the fore-edge should be ¹⁄₃₂" (fig. 7-8).

Fig. 7-8. Check fit of book in small tray.

In addition, the thickness of the book should be recessed ¹⁄₁₆" from the top edge of the small tray along the three walls (fig. 7-9).

We allow a little more flexibility with the clamshell box measurements than with the slipcase, because the book is fully enclosed by the two trays. Personal preference will dictate how much room to allow for spacing, but we usually prefer to err on the side of slightly greater margins for the clamshell box.

Fig. 7-9. Check depth of book in small tray.

PART II.
CONSTRUCT THE LID FOR
THE CLAMSHELL BOX

Step 1

Along with the three book board pieces for the lid, which include the front and back covers and spine, cut the two pieces of book cloth used for the outside and inside of the spine, two decorative papers, and two trim strips (fig. 7-10).

It is also helpful to have a set of spine-spacing guides available to place between the spine and the lid. Prepare two ³⁄₁₆" spacing guides (see chapter 2). This amount of spacing is recommended for the hinge between the spine and the lid boards. Note that this spacing is smaller than the spacing required for the book covers.

Fig. 7-10. Materials for constructing lid

Step 2

Place the book cloth so that the side to be glued is facing up. Using a ruler, find the exact midpoint across the width at the head and tail. Draw a light pencil line running the length, along the center. In addition, mark the head and tail of the spine board, indicating the exact midpoint. Apply PVA to the spine board on the opposite side that was marked in pencil (fig. 7-11).

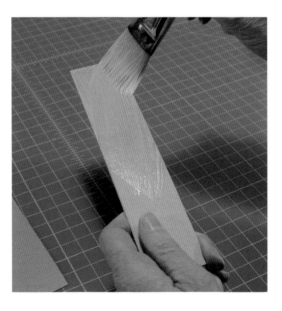

Fig. 7-11. Glue spine board instead of book cloth.

Proceed to place the spine board on the book cloth, centering it on the drawn line. At the same time, the spine board should also be centered between the head and tail of the book cloth, with a margin of approximately ⅝" allowed for the turn-in, while the margin between the spine board and the long edges is approximately 2" (fig. 7-12).

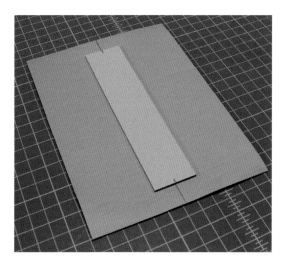

Fig. 7-12. Center spine on book cloth by using guide lines.

Step 3

Place a waste sheet under the book cloth and apply PVA to only one side of the book cloth. Be sure to hold the spine board firmly so the waste sheet does not shift (fig. 7-13).

After gluing the book cloth up to the edge of the spine, remove the waste sheet. Place two ³⁄₁₆" spacing guides directly against the bottom and top edges of the spine board, with the ends of the guides resting off the book cloth for easy removal. Next, set one of the two lid boards against the two spacing guides. Make sure the head and tail are lined up parallel with the head and tail of the spine piece (fig. 7-14).

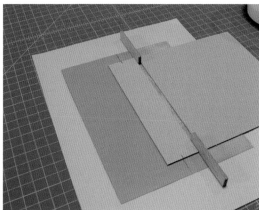

Fig. 7-13. Glue book cloth on one side of spine only.

Fig. 7-14. Use ³⁄₁₆" measuring guides for spacing.

Step 4

Attach the second lid board in the same manner. When completed, the two lid boards and spine board should be aligned evenly at the head and tail of the cover, with a ⅝" turn-in of book cloth extending beyond the boards (fig. 7-15).

Fig. 7-15. Attach second lid board.

Apply glue to the book cloth on the turn-ins both at the head and tail, and press them down onto the inside of the lid boards and spine pieces. Be sure to keep the book cloth snug along the edge of the board as you perform the turn-ins (fig. 7-16).

After both turn-ins are glued down, use the bone folder to assist you in pressing the book cloth into the hinge between the spine board and cover boards (fig. 7-17).

Turn the lid over and press into the joints, using your thumb or bone folder along the hinge to ensure that there is good contact on the outside of the book cloth (fig. 7-18).

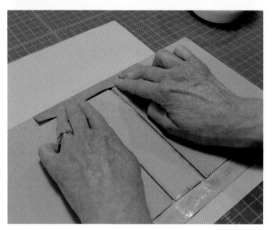

Fig. 7-16. Turn in book cloth over edge of boards.

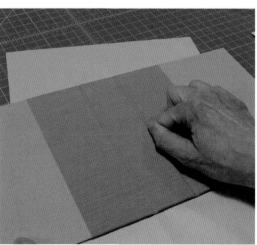

Fig. 7-17. Press on inside of hinges with bone folder.

Fig. 7-18. Press on outside of hinges with thumb.

Step 5

Glue the inside-spine book cloth piece onto the inside of the lid, centering it along the spine board. The head and tail of the book cloth spine should be recessed from the head and tail evenly, approximately ⅜" (fig. 7-19).

When gluing the book cloth spine piece, be sure to press down in the center of the spine first, then press the book cloth into the hinge by using the bone folder. Once good contact is made into the hinge with the bone folder, continue to press the book cloth onto the lid boards (fig. 7-20).

Fig. 7-19. Glue and center inside-spine book cloth.

Fig. 7-20. Press into hinges before pressing onto lid boards.

Step 6

Before adding the trim strip, you may need to square the book cloth to the fore-edge of the covers. See chapter 2 if you need to trim the book cloth to an even margin. To place the trim strip before adding the decorative paper, use a ruler or divider to measure and mark the book cloth 4" from the fore-edge. The mark should be made on both sides of the cover at the head and tail and should overlap the book cloth by ¼" (figs. 7-21 and 7-22).

Fig. 7-21. Measure from fore-edge for trim strip placement.

Fig. 7-22. A divider may be used for repeated measurements.

It is helpful to place the lid in a closed or angled position before applying the trim strip to the cover. Apply PVA to the trim strip and adhere it to the lid, using the 4" marks. When attaching the trim strip, line up carefully to cover the two marks and ensure it remains parallel to the spine. Allow for an even ⅝" turn-in at the head and tail on the inside of the cover boards (fig. 7-23).

Repeat this step on the other side of the lid.

Fig. 7-23. Attach decorative trim strip.

Step 7

To apply the decorative paper, measure 3¾" from the fore-edge. Mark on the trim strip at the head and tail, and on both sides of the lid. Glue the decorative paper over the trim strip so that it is aligned with and just covering the 3¾" marks. Ensure that the decorative paper is parallel to the trim strip and the spine. There should be an even ¼" margin of the trim strip evident. The three turn-ins at the head, tail, and fore-edge all should be approximately ⅝" (fig. 7-24).

Fig. 7-24. Attach decorative paper to lid.

Step 8

After positioning the decorative paper, turn the cover over and miter the two outside corners, using scissors. The cuts should be at a 45° angle, leaving a space from the corner to the cut lines of approximately ⅛", or 1½ times the thickness of the book board. Err on the side of having a little more margin when mitering corners. A mitered cut that is cut twice the book board thickness is usually safer than one that is less than 1½ the thickness. You can use a ⅛" measuring guide to ensure accuracy for this cut (figs. 7-25 and 7-26).

Fig. 7-25. Use scissors to miter corners.

Fig. 7-26. Corners mitered at 45° angle

Step 9

After both corners have been mitered, turn in the two short sides at the head and tail of the board, and press down onto the inside of the cover. If at any point the glue appears to be drying after making the mitered cuts, lightly reglue the turn-ins (fig. 7-27).

At both mitered corners, make a slight tuck that is down and inward before turning in the fore-edge. When making the corner tucks, we use our finger or a bone folder. This tuck is important to prevent a small burr from protruding at the corners (fig. 7-28).

After making the tuck, bring the long turn-in over the fore-edge of the board, and press down onto the inside of the cover. Smooth the corners by tapping them or applying gentle pressure with the bone folder (fig. 7-29).

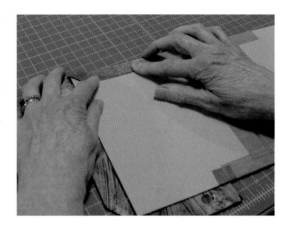

Fig. 7-27. Turn in two short sides onto inside of lid.

Fig. 7-28. Tuck in corners by using bone folder.

Fig. 7-29. Tap corners to gently round them.

Step 10

Repeat steps 6 through 9 on the other side to complete the attachment of the decorative papers. After both sides of the lid are covered, carefully smooth out the decorative papers, making sure there are no wrinkles (fig. 7-30).

Lay the lid flat with a pressing board and heavy weights on it. Separate the pressing board from the lid with a clean waste sheet or wax paper. Allow the lid to dry under weights for at least an hour, to prevent warping while you complete the trays (fig. 7-31).

Fig. 7-30. Finish both sides of lid.

Fig. 7-31. Place lid under press board and weights.

PART III.
COVER THE TWO TRAYS

Step 1

Organize the decorative papers into two sets for covering the two trays. Each set will contain four pieces, consisting of the tray bottom, one long wall, and two short walls. Since the pieces of both trays are similar in size, it is helpful to keep them separate or mark them on the back in light pencil with an "S" or "L," indicating the size (small and large) of each tray (fig. 7-32).

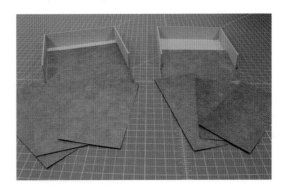

Fig. 7-32. Two trays with decorative papers

Step 2

Starting with the small tray, apply PVA to the paper used for the long wall. Center the back wall of the small tray on the paper so that there is an equal turn-in of ½" along the bottom of the tray and extending beyond the two short walls. There should also be about 2" extending from the top of the tray (fig. 7-33).

Wrap the paper around the two outside corners so that both the ½" turn-ins are glued onto the short tray walls. After this is completed, the corners of the paper will form a 90° angle, with a ½" turn-in below the tray (as in fig. 7-34) and a 2" turn-in above the tray (as in fig. 7-35). Help define the right angles at the four corners by creasing or gently pinching the corners with your thumb and forefinger (figs. 7-34 and 7-35).

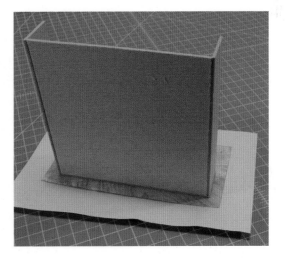

Fig. 7-33. Place outside back wall of small tray onto glued paper.

Fig. 7-34. Wrap paper onto two short walls.

Fig. 7-35. Define 90° angles at corners and extension above tray wall.

Step 3

Rotate the tray so you are looking at it from the bottom. Using your scissors, and from the outside of the tray, miter a "V" shape from the bottom corner turn-in. Elevate the scissors slightly to ensure you don't cut into the bottom corner of the tray (fig. 7-36).

Fig. 7-36. Make a "V"-shaped miter on bottom of tray.

Repeat this process with the other corner. These two mitered corners will create small tabs along the two short walls (fig. 7-37).

Fig. 7-37. Small tabs result from mitered "V" cut.

Step 4

Glue the two small tabs onto the tray bottom at each corner (fig. 7-38).

Fig. 7-38. Press two tabs onto bottom of tray.

Turn in the long edge of the long-wall paper onto the outside of the tray bottom, covering the short tab turn-ins (fig. 7-39).

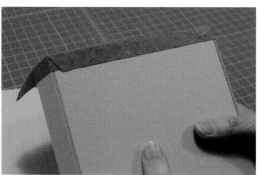

Fig. 7-39. Turn in long edge along bottom of tray.

Step 5

Rotate the tray so that you are looking down from the top of the tray at the inside corner. With the scissors positioned just to the inside of the short wall, make a cut straight down to the top edge of the board. The cut line should be recessed or offset ¹⁄₁₆" from the corner of the short wall (fig. 7-40).

This cut will create a long, narrow tab that will cover the inside corner of the tray (fig. 7-41).

Fig. 7-40. Cut line is slightly recessed from corner along inside wall.

Fig. 7-41. Corner tab and cut line are positioned just to inside of wall.

Step 6

Turn in the narrow tab onto the short tray wall and into the bottom corner of the tray. As you press the tab over the top edge of the tray, it will overlap both the long and short walls of the tray. It will also twist slightly at the top corner as the tab is brought downward.

Using your finger at first and then the bone folder, work the tab into the corner and onto the bottom of the tray. When completed, the tab will cover the corner of the tray from the top edge, down the inside both on the long and short walls, and onto the bottom of the tray. Use the bone folder to help press out the slight twist that occurs at the top corner. Complete this step at both corners of the tray (fig. 7-42).

Fig. 7-42. Work tab into corner and onto bottom of tray.

Step 7

Bring the long-wall turn-in over the top edge and onto the inner wall and the bottom of the tray. We will also make a very small mitered cut on the outside corners of the turn-in; however, be careful not to cut off too much, since it could leave a gap on the tray bottom (fig. 7-43).

Fig. 7-43. Small mitered cut on outside corners of turn-in

As you bring the turn-in over the top edge of the wall, this piece will neatly fit between the two short walls. At the same time, it will cover the narrow tab on the long wall. Use the bone folder along the corners to make a tight fit (fig. 7-44).

Normally, we prefer ⅝" or ¾" turn-ins, but because we are covering the inside bottom of the tray, we use a ½" turn-in. Along with the mitered cut, this narrower turn-in helps reduce the bulk in the corners.

Fig. 7-44. Turn in onto long wall then onto bottom of tray.

Step 8

Glue one of the short-wall papers to one of the tray's short walls. The paper should be placed so that it is recessed or offset ⅛" from the corner edge of the long wall and extends ½" past the front or open edge of the tray for the turn-in (fig. 7-45).

Fig. 7-45. Recess short-wall paper from back edge of tray.

The turn-ins should extend ½" along the bottom of the tray and, as with the long-wall paper, approximately 2" above the tray. Press down the turn-in onto the bottom of the tray. A 90° angle will form at the tray's front edge. Clearly define the right angle with your thumb and forefinger (fig. 7-46).

Fig. 7-46. Define 90° angle at front edge of tray.

Step 9

In this step you will make a series of three different cuts to cover the front edge of the tray.

Cut 1: Position the tray for the first cut so that the open end is facing you and you are holding the tray bottom in a vertical position. This will enable you to look straight down along the inside of the short wall of the tray. Make the cut toward the front edge of the short wall and recessed ¹⁄₁₆" from the bottom corner of the tray (fig. 7-47).

Fig. 7-47. **Cut 1** is toward front edge of short wall and recessed ¹⁄₁₆" from tray bottom.

This will produce a narrow tab that will cover the corner between the tray bottom and the short wall (fig. 7-48).

Fig. 7-48. Small tab that results from **cut 1**

Cut 2: Reposition the tray so your second cut is toward the top edge of the tray. The tray should be held in a vertical position but angled enough to allow you to make a straight cut with your scissors. It is important to recess the cut approximately 1/16" from the fore-edge of the short wall. Also, as you make this cut, STOP the cut 1/8" from the top edge of the board (fig. 7-49).

Cut 3: For the third cut, reposition the tray once again, this time so that it remains vertical, but you are looking at the front or open end of the tray. Make a diagonal cut from the top edge of the turn-in at the front edge of the tray, meeting precisely at the base of cut 2 (fig. 7-50).

The result after cut 3 will be two tabs used to cover the front edge of the tray, and the turn-in to cover the inside of the short wall (fig. 7-51).

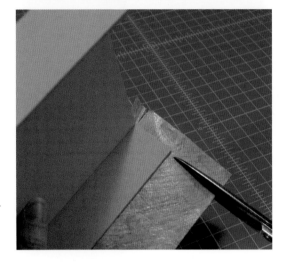

Fig. 7-49. **Cut 2** is from top of tray and 1/16" from fore-edge. Cut stops 1/8" from top edge of wall.

Fig. 7-50. **Cut 3** is at an angle from top edge of turn-in at front of tray and meets at base of **cut 2**.

Fig. 7-51. Set of three cuts creating three turn-ins

Step 10

After completing the cuts and as you are performing the turn-ins in this step, some light regluing may be needed.

First, turn in the small tab created from cut 1 over the front edge of the tray bottom, so that it twists slightly and overlaps both the short wall and the tray bottom (fig. 7-52).

Fig. 7-52. Turn in small tab to cover front bottom corner of tray.

Next, turn in the larger tab, resulting from cut 3, to cover the fore-edge of the short wall of the tray. This piece will neatly overlap the tab created from cut 1 on the bottom of the tray (fig. 7-53).

Fig. 7-53. Turn in short wall tab to cover front edge of tray wall.

Step 11

At the top corner of the front of the tray, where cut 2 meets cut 3, tuck in the paper with your finger or bone folder. This will eliminate a small burr that may form when turning in the paper onto the short wall (fig. 7-54).

Turn in the paper along the short wall and press down onto the tray bottom. When completed, the turn-in should be slightly recessed and neatly cover the large tab at the front edge of the tray (fig. 7-55).

Fig. 7-54. Tuck in corner at top edge of wall.

Fig. 7-55. Turn in onto short wall and onto bottom of tray.

Carefully use the bone folder to assist in pressing the paper along the bottom edge of the tray and into the corners (fig. 7-56).

Fig. 7-56. Use bone folder carefully in corners.

Step 12

Complete the covering of the second short wall of the tray in the same manner, repeating steps 8 through 11.

Step 13

Glue the small tray bottom paper to the inside of the small tray. Position the paper evenly at the back of the tray. Ensure that the paper is placed parallel to the back wall, so it does not angle onto the short walls of the tray when it is smoothed down onto the bottom of the tray (fig. 7-57).

Use the bone folder to press the paper down along the inner edges of the tray bottom (fig. 7-58).

Bring the tray bottom paper over the front edge of the tray and onto the outside bottom of the tray to complete (fig. 7-59).

Fig. 7-57. Glue and align paper on inside bottom of tray.

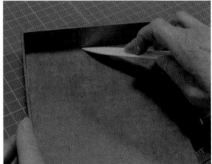

Fig. 7-58. Use bone folder to press down edges and corners.

Fig. 7-59. Bring turn-in onto outside bottom of tray.

Step 14

Repeat steps 2 through 13 to complete the covering of the large tray.

PART IV.
ATTACH THE TRAYS
TO THE LID

Step 1

Select the side that you prefer to be the top of the box, and mark the inside cover with an "A." The large tray (which is the top tray) should also be labeled on the bottom with an "A." Mark the small tray bottom and the inside of the opposite lid with a "B" (fig. 7-60).

Fig. 7-60. Label inside lids and bottoms of trays.

Fig. 7-61. Check alignment of trays before gluing.

Make a visual check of how the tray will be glued onto the lid, by positioning the tray so that the open end or front edge is placed toward the spine. The open edge should be aligned evenly with the edge of the lid along the hinge. The other three margins between the tray and lid should be evenly spaced (fig. 7-61).

Step 2

Apply a generous ¼" wide bead of PVA Thick to the bottom of the large tray. Using the thick-glue applicator, or a small brush, recess the bead of glue ½" from the four outer edges of the tray, to allow space for some spreading when the tray is pressed onto the lid (fig. 7-62).

Add additional PVA Thick to the middle area of the tray bottom, in a uniform pattern (fig. 7-63).

Fig. 7-62. Apply PVA Thick to bottom of large tray.

Fig. 7-63. Complete gluing with uniform pattern.

Step 3

PVA Thick, although quick drying, will allow enough time to properly position the tray. The margin around the three outside edges of the lid should be aligned evenly on each side of the lid, but it is more important that the open edge of the tray is lined up flush with the edge of the lid board along the spine. This even alignment of the trays ensures that the lid will close properly.

As described in step 1, position the large tray "A" onto the inside of lid "A" (fig. 7-64).

After gluing the first tray in place, add weights to the interior. The more evenly the weight is distributed, the better the contact between the tray and the lid. In addition, the heavier the weights, the better. The images show we used blocks of marble, just the right size for the tray. However, any combination of small weights that fit neatly into the corners of the tray will work.

Step 4

After completing the first tray, repeat steps 2 and 3 to attach the small tray "B." On the small tray, line up the open front end of the tray evenly with the spine edge of the lid board, as with the large tray. The small tray must be centered between the head and tail in order for the large tray to properly close, and nest over the small tray.

After the two trays are weighted, check for shifting and adjust if needed. Sometimes a slight shifting does occur, so always double-check before allowing the trays to dry overnight (see fig. 7-65).

The next day, we recommend that you close the clamshell box with your book placed inside. Place a press board on top of the closed box, with weights on top of the press board. Allow another twenty-four hours of drying time.

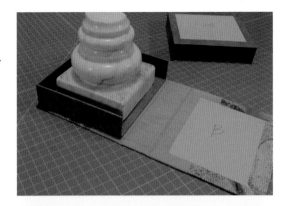

Fig. 7-64. Align front edge of tray flush with edge of spine board. Add weights.

Fig. 7-65. Add weights to small tray and dry overnight.

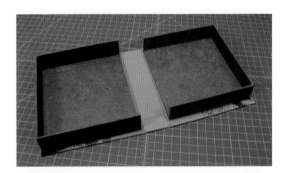

The completed Clamshell Box Project open and closed.

CHAPTER 8

Book and Box Making Formulas

There are several considerations before using the formulas listed below. The first item to point out is that the formulas are primarily guidelines to help you navigate the process of measuring and cutting your materials. They are not hard-and-fast rules regarding how to determine all your measurements. We usually use a combination of formulas, aesthetic considerations, and appropriate modifications. The modifications are based on such things as paper and book cloth thickness, grain direction, and flexibility regarding which measurements need to be precise and which ones can be rounded up or down.

We keep records of all our measurements and fine-tune them as needed. Record-keeping is a good practice and will help you in not only fine tuning your formulas, but to repeat them when needed. We also diagram our most popular patterns, so we can quickly see them. On our diagrams we usually list the width, height, grain direction, and the number of pieces we need to cut.

The second item to be considered is that the formulas listed in this chapter are intended for books and boxes that are constructed in a vertical or portrait orientation. If you are making a book or box in the horizontal or landscape orientation, such as a guest book or a landscape box, you will need to adjust the formulas to include modifications in grain direction as well as refine the measurements for margins. In these cases, the grain for covers will be parallel to the spine but run short.

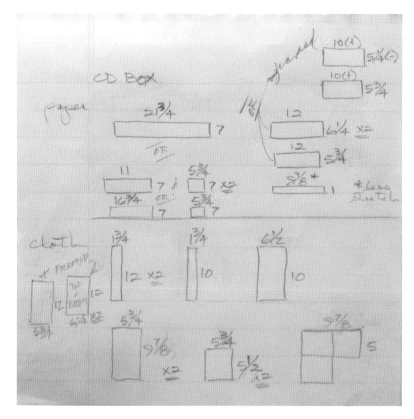

Record your measurements for reference.

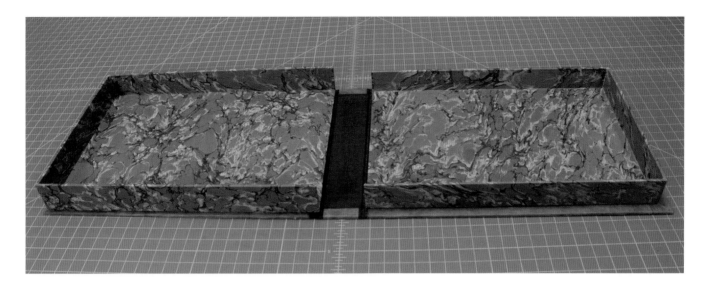

Finally, the formulas for each project include the following criteria:

1. Most of the formulas are written in a standard width (W) × length (L) format, and the width is the shorter dimension. However, we will sometimes substitute the thickness of the book or depth of the box for the width measurement. When this occurs, we use depth (D) to designate the measurement.

2. The starting point for calculating all the formulas is called the base measurement. When making books, the base measurement is determined by the dimensions of the text block. For slipcases and clamshell boxes, the base measurement is determined by the dimensions of the completed book and after it has been in the press, usually overnight. From these two sets of base measurements, specific formulas have been calculated for all the measurements required.

3. The grain direction in the formulas is indicated by the number that is underscored in each example listed under the formulas. Example: 5" × 7". The grain of the materials should run parallel to the number that is underscored.

4. There are some measurements that do not need to be precise to 1/32". These measurements, usually for paper or book cloth, are noted in the formula with an asterisk (*). This dimension may be rounded to the nearest 1/16". Note, however, that sometimes one measurement on a piece may be rounded, but the other must be precise. This occurs when a piece must fit between walls in one direction but has a turn-in on the other direction, as in the slipcase or clamshell tray bottoms.

In this chapter, we include how to measure a text block to determine the base measurements needed for determining the measurements of a case for the book. We also include how to determine the base measurement of a completed book to determine the base measurements needed for making a slipcase or clamshell box.

Landscape books and boxes will require adjustments to formulas.

155

PAMPHLET BOOK FORMULAS

PAMPHLET BOOK BASE MEASUREMENT

Text Block Width (W) _____ × Text Block Height (L) _____
    Example: 5½" × 8½"

Note: The pamphlet book formulas are designed for use with 8½" × 11" text paper that has been folded in half to form a text block with a measurement of 5½" × 8½".

The Pamphlet Book Project. See chapter 3 for complete instructions.

Decorative Paper Formulas

Flyleaf = (Text Block Width (W) × 2) + ⅛" _____ × Text Block Height (L) _____
    Example: 11⅛" × 8½"
    Quantity: 1

Note: The additional ⅛" is optional but is included to accommodate a slight fanning at the fore-edge of the folded text block. This fanning is especially noticeable with a thicker text block.

Cover Paper = Text Block Width (W) × 3.5 _____ × Text Block Height (L) + ⅛" _____
    Example: 19¼" × 8⅝"
    Quantity: 1

    OR

Optional Cover Paper = (Text Block Width (W) × 2) + ¼" _____ × Text Block Height (L) + ⅛" _____
    Example: 11¼" × 8⅝"
    Quantity: 1

FLAT-BACK BOOK FORMULAS

The formulas listed below are intended as guidelines for making your own custom flat-back books. They may call for some modifications, depending on the board thickness selected as well as personal and aesthetic considerations. The formulas for a flat-back book are generally suitable for a text block with a thickness of ⅛" to ¾". If your text block is over ¾" in thickness, we recommend making the round-back book.

The example measurements provided below for the formulas are based on using book board with a thickness of approximately .090 (³⁄₃₂") and a standard size 8½" × 11" text paper for the text block.

The Flat-Back Book Project. See chapter 4 for complete instructions.

CALCULATE THE HEIGHT, WIDTH, AND THICKNESS OF THE TEXT BLOCK

Begin by accurately recording the height, width, and spine thickness of your completed text block to determine the base measurement. The completed text block should include attached endpapers and super (spine reinforcement).

To measure the width and length of a text block, use a ruler with ¹⁄₁₆" calibrations. It is helpful to have a small square that can be set perpendicular against the head of the text block, as well as against the spine. To determine the width, measure the distance from the spine to the fore-edge and record to the nearest ¹⁄₁₆". To determine the height of the text block, measure the distance from the head to the tail and record to the nearest ¹⁄₁₆".

To determine the thickness of the spine of the text block, use a ruler and measure across the spine, recording to the nearest ¹⁄₁₆". Hold the text block firmly in your hand. Measure with a ruler or use a spring divider, then transfer this distance to a ruler. With either method, round to the nearest ¹⁄₁₆".

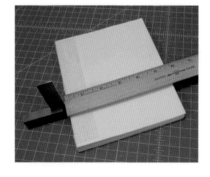
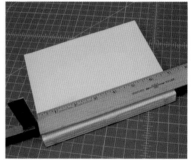

Measure the height and width of text block.

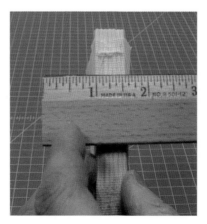

Measure spine thickness with ruler or spring divider.

FLAT-BACK BOOK BASE MEASUREMENT

Text Block Dimensions = Width (W) _____ × Height (L) _____ × Spine Thickness (D) _____
    Example: 5½" × 8½" × ⁵⁄₁₆"

Book Board Formulas

Book Covers = Text Block Width (W) _____ × Text Block Height (L) + ¼" _____
    Example: 5½" × 8¾"
    Quantity: 2

Spine Board = Text Block Spine Thickness (D) + ⅛"(+) _____ × Text Block Height (L) + ¼" _____
    Example: ⁷⁄₁₆"(+) × 8¾"
    Quantity: 1

Endpaper and Spine Formulas

Endpapers = Text Block Width (W) × 2 _____ × Text Block Height (L) _____
    Example: 11" × 8½"
    Quantity: 2

Super = Text Block Spine Thickness (D)* + 2¼" _____ × Text Block Height (L) − ½" _____
    Example: 2⅝" × 8"
    Quantity: 1

Headbands = Text Block Spine Thickness (D)* + ¼" _____
    Example: ⅝"
    Quantity: 2

Decorative Paper Formula

Decorative Paper = (Cover Board Width (W) × .75)* + ¾" _____ × Cover Board Height (L)* + 1½" _____
    Example: 4⅞" × 10¼"
    Quantity: 2

Book Cloth Formula

Book Cloth Spine = (Cover Board Width (W) × .50)* + Spine Board Width (D)* + ¾" _____ × Cover Board Height (L)* + 1½" _____
    Example: 4" × 10¼"
    Quantity: 1

ROUND-BACK BOOK FORMULAS

The formulas listed below are intended as guidelines for making your own round-back book. They may call for some modifications, depending on the board thickness selected as well as personal and aesthetic considerations. The formulas for a round-back book are generally suitable for a text block with a thickness of ¾" and over.

The example measurements provided below for the formulas are based on using book board with a thickness of approximately .090 (³⁄₃₂") and a standard size of 8½" × 11" text paper for the text block.

CALCULATE THE HEIGHT, WIDTH, AND THICKNESS OF THE TEXT BLOCK

Begin by accurately recording the height, width, and spine thickness of your completed text block to determine the base measurement. The completed rounded text block should include attached endpapers and super (spine reinforcement).

To measure the width and length of a text block, use a ruler with ¹⁄₁₆" calibrations. It is helpful to have a small square that can be set perpendicular against the head of the text block as well as against the spine. To determine the width, measure the distance from the spine to the fore-edge and record to the nearest ¹⁄₁₆". To determine the height of the text block, measure the distance from the head to the tail and record to the nearest ¹⁄₁₆".

The easiest way to accurately measure the thickness of a rounded spine is to use a narrow strip of scrap paper about 1" wide and several times longer than the spine width. Wrap the paper tightly across the spine and hold it firmly in place with your thumb and fingers. Use your other hand to crease the paper strip at the two edges of the spine, and mark them with a pencil. Lay this strip on a ruler to measure the distance between the two marks, rounding up or down to the nearest ¹⁄₁₆".

The Round-Back Book Project. See chapter 5 for complete instructions.

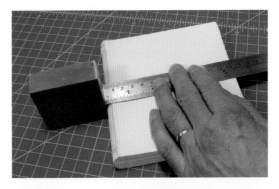

Use a square to measure rounded spine.

Use strip of paper to measure thickness of rounded spine.

ROUND-BACK BOOK BASE MEASUREMENT

Text Block Dimensions = Width (W) _____ × Height (L) _____ × Spine Thickness (D) _____
    Example: 5½" × <u>8½"</u> × 1"

Spine Formulas

Endpaper = (Text Block Width (W) × 2) _____ × Text Block Height (L) _____
    Example: 11" × <u>8½"</u>
    Quantity: 2

Protective Wrap = Text Block Width (W)* + 2 _____ × Text Block Height (L)* × 2.5 _____
    Example: <u>7½"</u> × 21¼"
    Quantity: 1

Super = Text Block Thickness (D)* + 2½" _____ × Text Block Height (L) – ½" _____
    Example: 3½" × <u>8"</u>
    Quantity: 1

Spine Lining = Text Block Thickness (D) – 1/16" _____ × Text Block Height (L) – 1 1/16" _____
    Example: 15/16" × <u>7 7/16"</u>
    Quantity: 1

Headbands = Text Block Thickness (D)* + ¼" _____
    Example: 1¼"
    Quantity: 2

Hollow Tube = (Text Block Thickness (D) × 3) – 1/16" _____ × Text Block Height (L) _____
    Example: 2 15/16" × <u>8½"</u>
    Quantity: 1

Book Board and Spine Inlay Formulas

Book Covers = Text Block Width (W) _____ × Text Block Height (L) + ¼" _____
    Example: 5½" × <u>8¾"</u>
    Quantity: 2

Spine Inlay = Text Block Thickness (D) + 1/16" _____ × Text Block Height (L) + ¼" _____
    Example: 1 1/16" × <u>8¾"</u>
    Quantity: 1

Decorative Paper Formulas

Decorative Paper = (Book Board Width (W) × .60)* + ¾" _____ × Book Board Height (L)* + 1½" _____
    Example: 4" × <u>10¼"</u>
    Quantity: 2

Trim Strip = Width ¾" × Book Board Height (L)* + 1½" _____
    Example: ¾" × <u>10¼"</u>
    Quantity: 2

Book Cloth Formula

Book Cloth Spine = (Book Board Width (W) × .80)* + Text Block Thickness (D)* + ½" _____ × Book Board Height (L)* + 1½" _____
    Example: 6" × 10¼"
    Quantity: 1

SLIPCASE FORMULAS

The formulas listed below are intended as guidelines for making your own custom slipcase. They may call for some modifications, depending on the board thickness selected as well as personal and aesthetic considerations. The formulas for the slipcase can be used to hold any size of book, including the round-back.

Keep in mind that the thickness for the inside lining should closely match the paper that is being used to cover the outside, to help prevent warping. The common thickness helps equalize tension on both sides of the board after it dries. The formulas are designed to use a medium-weight 70 lb. / 105 gsm text paper, with a range of 60 lb. / 90 gsm to 80 lb. / 120 gsm being usable. If the lining paper is significantly thicker or thinner, it can affect the fit of the book in the slipcase.

The example measurements provided below for the formulas are based on using book board with a thickness of approximately .090 (³⁄₃₂") and a standard size of 8½" × 11" text paper for the text block.

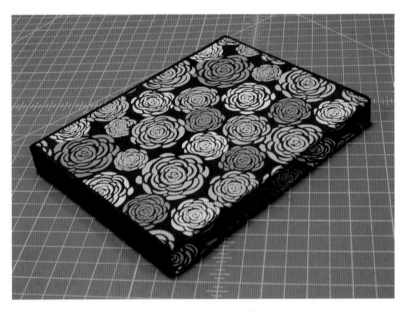

The Slipcase Project. See chapter 6 for complete instructions.

CALCULATE THE HEIGHT, WIDTH, AND THICKNESS OF THE BOOK

Before cutting the board pieces for a slipcase, you will need to determine the measurements of your book. Begin by recording, as accurately as possible, the height, width, and spine thickness of the completed, dry, and pressed book.

To determine the width, measure from the spine to the fore-edge of the book. Using a square against the spine is especially effective if you are attempting to obtain the width measurement for a round-back book. Measure and record the width, rounding up to the nearest ¹⁄₃₂".

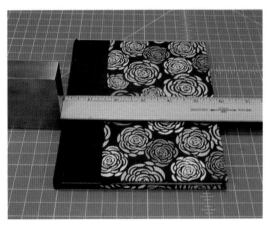

Measure width of finished book.

To accurately measure the height of a book, place a small steel square so that it is flush against the head or tail. Lay a ruler across the book cover from the head to tail. Measure and record the height, again rounding up to the nearest ¹⁄₃₂".

Set a squared piece of book board with the edge set against the spine of the book. Using a thin, metal ruler or thin straightedge, lay the ruler across the width of the book and then place a pencil mark where it meets the book board. In the same manner, check a couple of additional measurements along the head or tail near the spine, to ensure that the thickness is consistent, and use the largest number. A divider may be used to obtain this measurement as well.

Measure height of finished book.

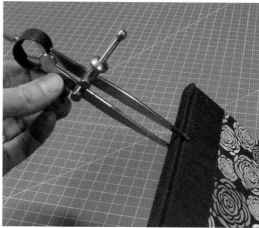

Measure spine thickness with squared board and straightedge or with spring divider.

SLIPCASE BOOK BASE MEASUREMENT

Book Dimensions = Width (W) _____ × Height (L) _____ × Spine Thickness (D) _____
    Example: 5¹³⁄₁₆" × <u>8¾"(+)</u> × ½"(+)

Book Board Formulas

Front/Back Side Panels = Book Width (W) + ⅛" _____ × Book Height (L) + ¼" _____
    Example: 5¹⁵⁄₁₆" × <u>9"(+)</u>
    Quantity: 2

Spine Wall = Book Thickness (D) + ¹⁄₁₆" _____ × Front/Back Side Panel Height (L) _____
    Example: ⁹⁄₁₆"(+) × <u>9"(+)</u>
    Quantity: 1

Head/Tail Wall = Book Thickness (D) + ¹⁄₁₆" _____ × Front/Back Side Panel Width (W) – ³⁄₃₂" _____
    Example: ⁹⁄₁₆"(+) × 5⅞"(–)
    Quantity: 2

Lining Paper Formulas

Front/Back Side Panel = Panel Board Width (W)* + 1"_____ × Panel Board Length (L)* + 1" _____
    Example: 7" × 10"
    Quantity: 2

Spine Wall = Spine Wall Board Depth (D)* + 1" _____ × Spine Wall Board Height (L)* + 1" _____
    Example: 1⅝" × 10"
    Quantity: 1

Head/Tail Wall = Head/Tail Wall Board Depth (D)* + 1"_____ × Head/Tail Board Height (L)* + 1" _____
    Example: 1⅝" × 6⅞"
    Quantity: 2

Book Cloth Formulas

Spine Wall = Spine Wall Board Depth (D)* + 1¼" _____ × Spine Wall Board Height (L)* + 1¼" _____
    Example: 1⅞" × 10¼"
    Quantity: 1

Head/Tail Wall = Head/Tail Wall Board Depth (D)* + 1¼" _____ × Head/Tail Wall Height (L)* + ½" _____
    Example: 1⅞" × 6½"
    Quantity: 2

Decorative Paper Formula

Front/Back Panel Decorative Paper = Panel Board Width (W)* + ½" _____ × Panel Board Height (L) – ¼" _____
    Example: 6½" × 8¾"(+)
    Quantity: 2

CLAMSHELL BOX FORMULAS

The formulas listed below are intended as guidelines for making your own custom clamshell box. They may call for some modifications, depending on the board thickness selected as well as personal and aesthetic considerations. The formulas for the clamshell box can be used to hold any size of book.

The example measurements provided for the formulas are based on using book board with a thickness of approximately .090 ($\frac{3}{32}$").

The Clamshell Box Project. See chapter 7 for complete instructions.

CALCULATE THE HEIGHT, WIDTH, AND THICKNESS OF THE BOOK

Before cutting the board pieces for a clamshell box, you will need to determine the measurements of your book. Begin by recording, as accurately as possible, the height, width, and spine thickness of the completed, dry, and pressed book.

To determine the width, measure from the spine to the fore-edge of the book. Using a square against the spine is especially effective if you are attempting to obtain the width measurement for a round-back book. Measure and record the width, rounding up to the nearest $\frac{1}{16}$".

Measure width of finished book.

To accurately measure the height of a book, place a small steel square so that it is flush against the head or tail. Lay a ruler across the book cover from the head to tail and measure and record the height, again rounding up to the nearest $\frac{1}{16}$".

Set a squared piece of book board with the edge set against the spine of the book. Using a thin, metal ruler or thin straightedge, lay the ruler across the cover along the width of the book and then place a pencil mark where it meets the book board. In the same manner, check a couple of additional measurements along the head or tail near the spine, to ensure the thickness is consistent, and use the largest number. A spring divider may be used to obtain this measurement as well.

Measure height of finished book.

Measure spine thickness with squared board and straightedge or with spring divider.

CLAMSHELL BOX BASE MEASUREMENT

Book Dimensions = Width (W) _____ × Height (L) _____ × Spine Thickness (D) _____
    Example: 5⅞" × <u>8¾"</u> × ⅞"

Book Board Formulas

Small Tray Bottom = Book Width (W) + 1/16" _____ × Book Height (L) + ⅛" _____
    Example: 5¹⁵/₁₆" × <u>8⅞"</u>
    Quantity: 1

Small Tray Long Wall = Book Spine Thickness (D) + 3/16" _____ × Small Tray Bottom Length (L) + 3/16" _____
    Example: 1¹/₁₆" × <u>9¹/₁₆"</u>
    Quantity: 1

Small Tray Short Wall = Book Spine Thickness (D) + 3/16" _____ × Small Tray Bottom Width (W) _____
    Example: 1¹/₁₆" × <u>5⁵/₁₆"</u>
    Quantity: 2

Large Tray Bottom = Small Tray Bottom Width (W) + 3/16" _____ × Small Tray Bottom Length (L) + 5/16" _____
    Example: 6⅛" × <u>9³/₁₆"</u>
    Quantity: 1

Large Tray Long Wall = Small Tray Height (D) + 3/16" _____ × Large Tray Bottom (L) + 3/16" _____
    Example: 1¼" × <u>9⅜"</u>
    Quantity: 1

Large Tray Short Wall = Small Tray Height (D) + 3/16" _____ × Large Tray Bottom Width (W) _____
    Example: 1¼" × <u>6⅛"</u>
    Quantity: 2

Lid = Large Tray Bottom Width (W) + 5/16" _____ × Large Tray Bottom Length (L) + 9/16" _____
    Example: 6⁷/₁₆" × <u>9¾"</u>
    Quantity: 2

Spine = Large Tray Long Wall Height (D) + 1/16" _____ × Lid Length (L) _____
    Example: 1⁵/₁₆" × <u>9¾"</u>
    Quantity: 1

Decorative Paper Formulas

Small Tray Bottom = Small Tray Bottom Width (W)* + ¾" _____ × Small Tray Bottom Length (L) − ⅛" _____
    Example: 6¾" × <u>8¾"</u>
    Quantity: 1

Small Tray Long Wall = (Small Tray Height (D) × 2)* + ⅞" _____ × Small Tray Long Wall Length (L)* + 1" _____
    Example: 3" × <u>10⅛"</u>
    Quantity: 1

Small Tray Short Wall = (Small Tray Height (D) × 2)* + ⅞" _____ × Small Tray Short Wall Length (L)* + ½" _____
    Example: 3" × <u>6½"</u>
    Quantity: 2

Large Tray Bottom = Large Tray Bottom Width (W)* + ¾" _____ × Large Tray Bottom Length (L) – ⅛" _____
    Example: 6⅞" × <u>9¹/₁₆"</u>
    Quantity: 1

Large Tray Long Wall = (Large Tray Height (D) × 2)* + ⅞" _____ × Large Tray Long Wall Length (L)* + 1" _____
    Example: 3⅜" × <u>10⅜"</u>
    Quantity: 1

Large Tray Short Wall = (Large Tray Height (D) × 2)* + ⅞" _____ × Large Tray Short Wall Length (L)* + ½" _____
    Example: 3⅜" × <u>6⅝"</u>
    Quantity: 2

Lid = (Lid Board Width (W) × .60)* + ¾" _____ × Lid Board Length (L)* + 1½" _____
    Example: 4⅝" × <u>11¼"</u>
    Quantity: 2

Trim Strip = Width ¾" × Lid Board Length (L)* + 1½" _____
    Example: ¾" × <u>11¼"</u>
    Quantity: 1

Book Cloth Formulas

Outside Spine = (Lid Board Width (W) × .80)* + Spine Board Depth (D)* + ½" _____ × Spine Board Length (L)* + 1½" _____
    Example: 7⅛" × <u>11¼"</u>
    Quantity: 1

Inside Spine = Spine Board Depth (D)* + 2" _____ × Small Tray Bottom Length (L) + ¹/₁₆" _____
    Example: 3⅜" × <u>8¹⁵/₁₆"</u>
    Quantity: 1

Gallery of Books and Boxes

A collection of books and boxes by Tom and Cindy Hollander

All the books and boxes shown in the gallery chapter were made by Tom and Cindy Hollander. Where hand-marbled papers were used or others were involved, we tried to give credit to the artists or instructors as best we could.

We enjoy using elegant decorative papers for endpapers such as the marbled endpaper shown here. This blank journal contains six signatures and ninety-six pages. Somerset Book text paper with the deckle edges evident at the fore-edge of the book adds interest.

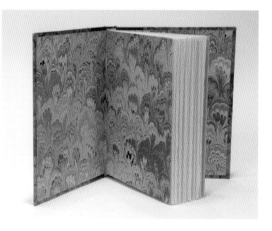

A traditional flat-back book. 5½" × 7" × ¾"

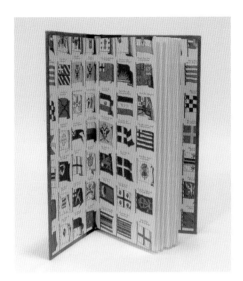

A flat-back book with endsheets of Florentine print flags of the world.
4" × 10" × ¾"

An open book with fanned text pages is an architecturally pleasing view. In this example, a mauve-colored *chiri* tissue-weight paper from Thailand is included with each signature, forming separate sections throughout the book.

A silver Japanese book cloth is used for the spines of this book and box set. A parrot-green *lokta* paper from Nepal is used for the two trays, trim strips, and endpapers. A gray-and-white French marbled paper covers the book and box.

Flat-back book with fanned text pages.
4¼" × 11" × ¾"

Flat-back book with clamshell box.
Book 5¾" × 7" × ¾",
clamshell box 6½" × 8¼" × 1"

A collection of
round-back books.
5¼" × 5¾" × 1"

We use a variety of decorative papers, book cloths, and endpapers in our round-back books. The books contain twelve signatures each of Somerset Book text and have 200 pages. Many of these books were made as examples while teaching workshops.

A zebra print *lokta* paper from Nepal is used for endpapers, and a decorative trim strip is used on the front covers of this round-back book. The use of a black-and-white checkered headband accents the design. The outside spine is a coral imitation suede, while the decorative paper on the covers is a Japanese *chiyogami* paper.

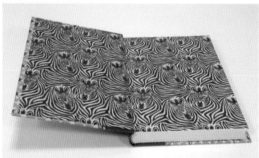

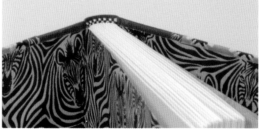

The Zebra
round-back book.
5¾" × 8¾" × 1"

This round-back book uses a marbled paper handmade by Galen Berry that he calls Dragons in the Sky. The book cloth is a paper-backed Italian cloth known as Cialux. The endpapers and trim strip are a handmade *lokta* paper from Nepal. A red-and-yellow headband complements the colors of the book.

Dragons in the Sky round-back book.
5¼" × 5¾" × 1"

This large leather-bound book is called a tight back because the spine of the text block is glued directly to the leather spine. The library-style binding includes goat leather corners and split boards to make it durable. The signatures are sewn onto thick cords before attaching to the covers. This structure was taught to us by head conservator Jim Craven, Bentley Library, University of Michigan.

Leather library-style binding.
6½" × 10½" × 2"

Our guest book has helped us celebrate several store anniversaries over a twenty-five-year period. It is composed of three signatures and sixty pages and uses a ½" wide spine inlay of book cloth. We added a gold Momi paper trim strip with the deckle edge placed against burgundy Japanese book cloth on the covers. The hand-painted dragonfly and overmarbled paper is a classic design of Moth Marblers.

This portfolio box with ribbon ties is essentially a clamshell box. It is ideal for holding prints, photographs, documents, or loose papers. The box includes a handmade Richard Langdell paper with the deckle edge overlapping Japanese book cloth. The two trays feature a Japanese *chiyogami* paper with traditional cranes-in-flight motif.

Anniversary guest book.
6" × 10¼" × ½"

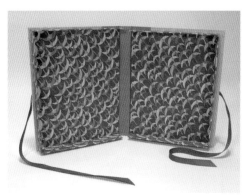

Portfolio box with ribbon ties.
9" × 12" × 1"

Pamphlet books taught to students in a college writing class serve as a collection of their stories. The turned-in decorative cover papers of the books allow them to stand upright so they can be displayed as presented here.

The goat leather spine is the dominant feature on this thick hand-sewn book, using printed signatures written by book artist Keith Smith.

The goat leather is split thin so that it is workable without having to pare it. Applying narrow and tapered ¼" strips (faux bands) of leather under the spine gives this book the appearance of having been sewn on cords. The printed decorative paper comes from Bomo in Hungary. This structure was taught to us by Jon Buller, former owner of the Bessenberg Bindery in Ann Arbor.

A collection of pamphlet books.
5½" × 8½" × ¼"

Leather round-back book of Non-adhesive Binding, by Keith Smith.
6¼" × 9" × 2"

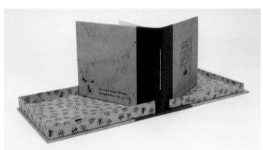

Watch Out for Ants!, by Jessica Hollander. Book 4¼" × 5½" × ¼", clamshell box 5" × 6" × ½"

Watch Out for Ants! is a story about saving a sidewalk ant colony. The book is a hard cover single-signature pamphlet book with sewing through the book cloth spine. The ant paper is from India and is used for the endpapers and to cover the trays. The reverse side of the paper is used for the cover of the book and box. The title design is set on the covers as an onlay, using black book cloth as a border.

This elegant flat-back book and clamshell box was made as part of a workshop we taught in 2018. It highlights a Japanese *chiyogami* paper, Japanese book cloth, and coral-colored imitation suede. The text block is a soft cream-colored Somerset Book paper and contains ninety-six pages.

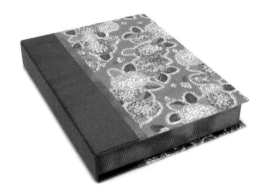

Flat-back book with clamshell box. Book 5½" × 7" × ¾", clamshell box 5¾" × 7¼" × 1"

A traditional Italian wood block design is used on the covers for two slipcases and books, creating two different styles. One slipcase utilizes an evergreen Bugra paper and smaller design element onlay, framed on yellow book cloth. The second slipcase frames a much-larger design component over the Bugra paper.

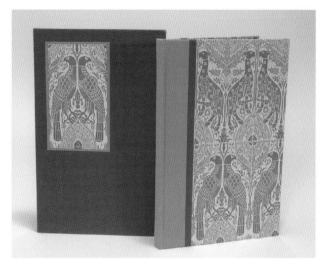

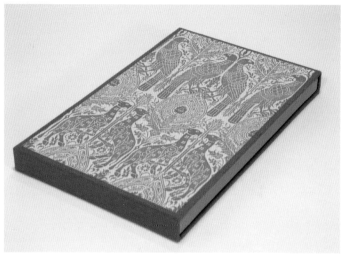

Flat-back books with differing slipcase designs. Book 6" × 9" × 1", slipcase 6¼" × 9¼" × 1"

This stylish slipcase with six small flat-back books is made using Teagan and Ashe papers that are hand-decorated with splashes of metallic paints.

Slipcase with six flat-back books. Books 4½" × 5" × ¾", slipcase 4" × 5¼" × 6"

The corkskin flat-back and slipcase set illustrates how we often use the endpaper of the book to line the inside of a slipcase, creating an unexpected complement. The cover of the book and slipcase feature mosaic corkskin paper from Portugal and Japanese book cloth. The dragonfly paper used for the endpaper and lining is from Florence.

Corkskin flat-back book
and slipcase.
Book 5½" × 7" × ¾",
slipcase 5¾" × 7¼" × 1"

Tight-back leather-bound book.
5¼" × 6¾" × 1½"

The use of rich Harmatan goat leather along the spine and fore-edge complements the exquisite hand-marbled paper from France applied to the cover of this tight-back book. Blind tooling with a bone folder etches a distinctive border along each edge of the papers.

Black-and-red geometric Japanese *chiyogami* paper is the focal point of this flat-back and slipcase set. The deep-red *lokta* for the endpapers and solid-red headbands tie the two together. The text block is ninety-six pages and utilizes the soft and luxuriant Somerset Book text paper.

Flat-back book and slipcase.
Book 5½" × 7" × ¾",
slipcase 5¾" × 7¼" × 1"

Our Box in a Box features a clamshell-style lid, a shallow tray, and a compartment below the tray to store a second box or even a book. The design is from a Florentine paper and is an image of Florence during the Middle Ages. The lids and outer box are covered in an Alvey Jones, Open Sky handmade paper. A ribbon tab on the smaller box is used to pull the box out of its compartment.

This little flat-back book with crocodile motif makes a perfect gift. The crocodile paper is from Zimbabwe, and the paper used for end-papers, trim strips, and trays is from India.

Box in a Box.
Small hinged-lid box 7½" × 9¼" × 1", large clamshell box 9" × 11" × 3"

Crocodile flat-back book with clamshell box.
Book 4½" × 5½" × ¾", clamshell box 5" × 6" × 1"

Prototype of custom photo album and clamshell box.
Album 11¾" × 13½" × 1¼", clamshell box 12" × 14" × 1½"

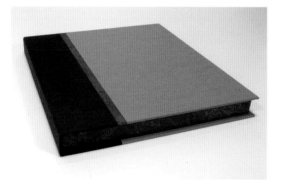

We were commissioned to make a special book-and-box set to be presented to President Gerald Ford by the University of Michigan. This prototype includes an embossed paper emblem inlay of the university seal. After it was completed, it was replaced with a gold medallion. The book and clamshell box utilize a rich bronze-and-blue Japanese book cloth, and the blue-and-gold French marbled paper echo the university's colors.

The caterpillar stitch was invented by Betsy Palmer Eldridge and made famous by book artist and author Keith Smith. This book clearly illustrates how a collection of signatures are sewn into the spine in this intriguing nonadhesive binding.

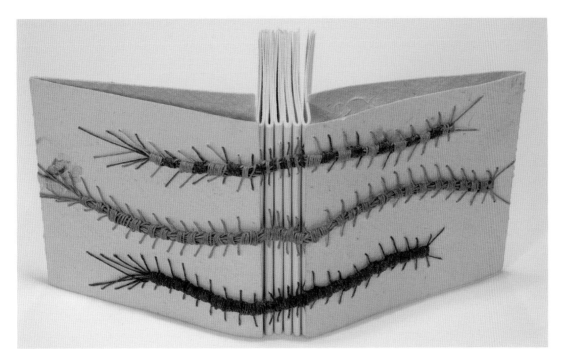

Caterpillar Stitch book.
4¼" × 10½" × 1"

This round-back book is housed in a slipcase with a rounded fore-edge. The process is similar to our slipcase project, except that the rounded opening needs to be cut and shaped to the spine of the book. A series of narrow tabs are required, along with a good deal of finesse to neatly cover a rounded edge.

Round-back book with rounded slipcase.
Book 5½" × 5¾" × 1",
slipcase 5¾" × 6" × 1¼"

A classic Japanese *chiyogami* paper and metallic Indian paper combine with a black mohair Japanese book cloth to produce this elegant set comprising a round-back book and clamshell box.

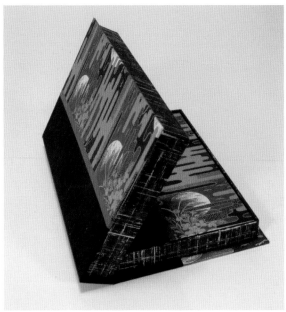

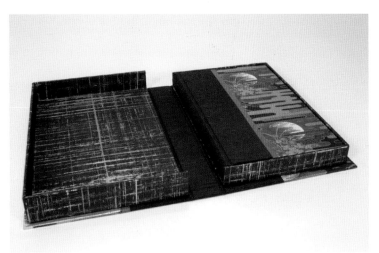

Round-back with clamshell box.
Book 5¾" × 8¾" × ¾", clamshell box 6" × 9" × 1"

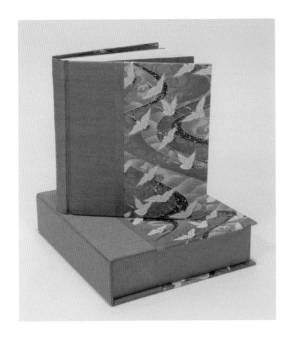

Using a Florentine paper with a Picasso-like design, we cased-in a small lined journal and set it in a matching slipcase. The slipcase onlay is bordered with green-starched linen book cloth. The Japanese book cloth on the spine and slipcase is a blue-silver rayon that has a silklike quality.

Round-back book with clamshell box.
Book 5½" × 6" × 1",
clamshell box
6" × 6½" × 1¼"

Lined flat-back book with slipcase.
Book 3½" × 5½" × ¾",
slipcase 3¾" × 5¾" × 1"

A glimpse of decorative paper against the solid-colored book cloth spine is evident when placing a round-back book in a rectangular slipcase. In this book and slipcase, we used a hand-marbled paper by Galen Berry, appropriately called Space Odyssey.

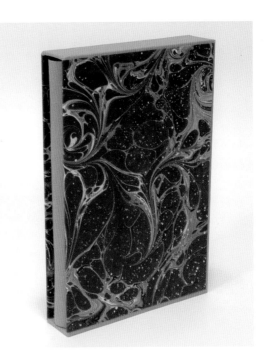

Space Odyssey round-back book with slipcase.
Book 5¾" × 8¾" × 1¼",
slipcase 6" × 8" × 1½"

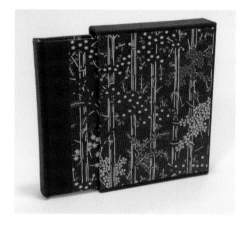

This small flat-back book and slipcase are made with burgundy Japanese book cloth and Japanese *chiyogami* paper. The endpaper and slipcase lining are a subtle Japanese motif in green that matches the green color on the decorative paper. The book contains ninety-six pages of high-quality Arches Text Wove paper.

The single-sheet sewing book is a nonadhesive binding sewn across the spine by using four needles and waxed thread. Artists appreciate the unfolded single sheets to display their artwork. This style is especially functional as a photo album that lies flat when opened.

Small flat-back book
with slipcase.
Book 4" × 5" × ¾",
slipcase 4¼" × 5¼" × 1"

Single-sheet sewing.
5¼" × 8½" × 1"

This decorative and functional four-panel table-top screen is made by using four pieces of 4¾" × 12½" book board attached by a hinged spine in the same fashion as making a lid for a box.

Along with narrow strips of book cloth for the hinges, we selected a Moth Marble original paper for one side and a *lokta* Nepalese paper for the other side of the screen.

Four-panel table top screen.
12½" × 19"

Our chap book and box sets are made by using a standard 8½" × 11" text paper and cutting it in half to produce 4¼" × 5½" folios. We have produced a kit of precut book board pieces, making it easy to print, bind, and present custom content.

Chap books with clamshell box.
Books 4½" × 5¾" × ½",
clamshell boxes
4¾" × 6" × ¾"

This handsome burgundy leather journal incorporates sturdy endcaps that cover the sewn headbands. The paper is from England and was handmade by Ann Muir, whose marbled papers were used in some of the *Harry Potter* movies.

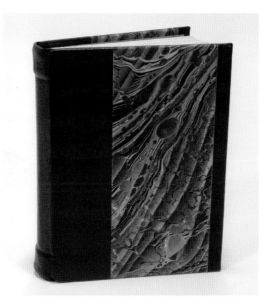

Leather tight-back book.
5½" × 6¾" × 1½"

Historical sewing sampler with clamshell box.
Book 4" × 11¼" × ¾",
clamshell box
4¼" × 11½" × 1"

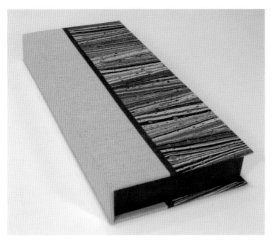

To house a sewing sampler that was taught at a Hollander's workshop by historical-binding scholar Julia Miller, we made a special clamshell box. A unique Chena River Marblers paper spoke to us for this box (it said, "Use me for this box!"). A linen-style Japanese book cloth and burgundy *lokta* paper for the trays and trim strip enhance the unfinished book.

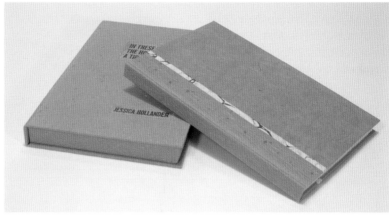

This clamshell box is made to house our daughter's first book. We cut and peeled off the book board to create two title inlays that are letterpress printed. The book cloth is a paper-backed Chinese brocade design, and the endpapers are a hand marble by Iris Nevins.

An example of a leather-bound book features sewing the text block on cords. The paper is from our extensive collection of Moth Marbles. Inside the book is an orange Ingres paper as endpapers. Orange and brown threads are used to sew the headbands.

In These Times the Home Is a Tired Place, by Jessica Hollander, with clamshell box. Book 6" × 9¼" × ½", clamshell box 6¼" × 9½" × ¾"

Leather-bound tight-back book. 4¾" × 6¼" × 1½"

This hard cover pamphlet book uses a map of the Spanish coastline for the endpapers. These small, single-signature books make excellent travel journals.

The millimeter binding was taught to us by Don Etherington, world-renowned fine binder and conservator. The millimeter refers to the use of a very thin strip of leather at the head and tail edges of the case. It was developed as a binding style during World War II to conserve fine binding leather. The slipcase is made using a complementary hand-marbled paper from France.

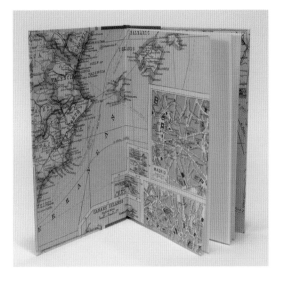

Pamphlet map book.
5¾" × 8¾" × ¼"

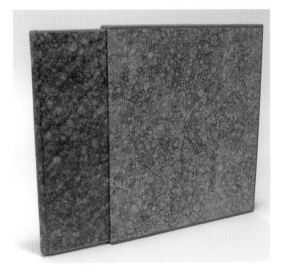

Millimeter binding
with slipcase.
Book 8¼" × 9¼" × ½",
slipcase 8½" × 9½" × ¾"

This set consisting of a clamshell box and round-back book uses a hand-marbled paper made by Iris Nevins. The two trays and trim are covered in Bugra, a paper manufactured in Germany.

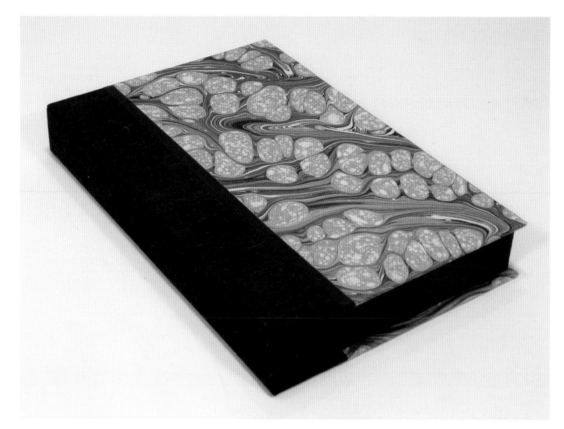

Round-back book with clamshell box.
Book 5¾" × 8¾" × ¾",
clamshell box
6½" × 9½" × 1"

We made this round-back to fit perfectly in a square box, just to prove it can be done! To highlight the paper and book cloth contrast, a Japanese black mohair with gold threads complements the hand-marbled paper by Chena River Marblers. An orange *lokta* is used as the endpapers, and orange-and-yellow headbands provide the finishing touch.

Round-back book with slipcase.
Book 4½" × 5" × 1",
slipcase 4¾" × 5" × 1¼"

This flat-back book is made with a goat leather spine and corners. It also features very thin leather headbands placed over a thin core. Blind tooling along the edges of the leather is evident where it meets the decorative paper. The text block is constructed with six signatures of Somerset Book paper.

Flat-back book
with corners.
5½" × 7¼" × ¾"

The Tiger Eye is a hand-marbled paper by Renato Crepaldi from Brazil. It is the inspiration for this small set comprising a round-back book and clamshell box. The orange *lokta* paper from Nepal is a perfect complement for covering the trays and trim strip.

Round-back book with clamshell box.
Book 4¼" × 5¼" × 1",
clamshell box
4¾" × 5½" × 1½"

A black-and-white house paper is used on the covers of this slipcase and flat-back book. It was selected to complement the theme of the book, which is about a teenager growing up in suburbia. A sage-green *lokta* paper is used to cover the entire slipcase and as a trim strip and endpapers on the book.

House Paper flat-back book with slipcase.
Book 5¾" × 8¾" × ¾",
slipcase 6" × 9" × 1"

This nonadhesive binding is known as the Secret Belgian Binding because it had remained a mystery until the sewing technique was unraveled by book artist Hedi Kyle. The exposed sewing consists of a woven pattern holding the covers and text block to the spine. The text block, sewn separately, is incorporated into the cover with the aid of paper tapes.

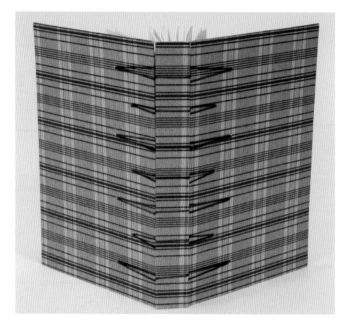

Secret Belgian binding.
4¼" × 6" × ¾"

This flat-back book and slipcase use ivory amate bark paper handmade by the Otomi Indian culture in Mexico. The slipcase features an onlay of a rich Galen Berry hand-marbled paper over a wide strip of brown amate bark. The vibrancy of the marbled paper is repeated with the endpapers.

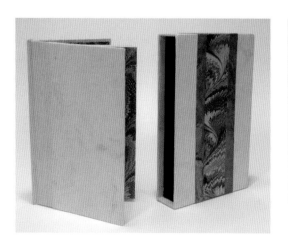

Amate bark flat-back book and slipcase.
Book 6" × 9¼" × ¾",
slipcase 6¼" × 9½" × 1½"

Three hard cover pamphlet books fit into the slipcase, which is completely covered in Japanese book cloth. Casing-in a single-signature booklet utilizes a soft spine of book cloth and endpapers that are tipped-in onto the signature. The marbled papers are produced by Bohemio Bindery and Galen Berry.

Three pamphlet books with slipcase.
Books 5¾" × 8¾" × ¼", slipcase 9" × 6" × 1"

This single-sheet book art structure illustrates a more advanced exposed sewing style. It is sewn across the spine by using waxed thread and three needles. The stitching highlights an Indian paper onlay with additional embroidery on the cover.

Single-sheet sewing.
4½" × 7" × 1½"

Bare Birch is a *lokta* paper from Nepal and was the inspiration for this flat-back book. The text block is ninety-six pages and utilizes 70 lb. Oatmeal Speckletone text paper.

Bare Birch flat-back book.
Book 5½" × 7" × ¾"

The Swimming Trout box opens into a divided tray with a clamshell-style lid. A unique feature of this box is a wide elastic band that is glued under the top lid and wraps around the bottom of the box, to hold it securely closed. The paper is a wood block print from India with *lokta* paper from Nepal for the box and lid lining.

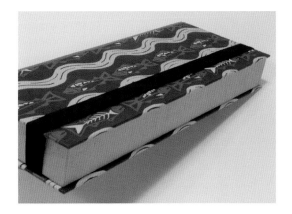

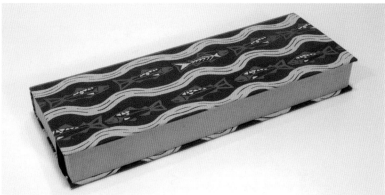

Swimming Trout box.
5" × 14" × 1½"

The exposed sewing style of the butterfly stitch, as taught by Keith Smith, is used in this pamphlet book. The sewing across the spine includes two different colors of waxed thread. Red Harmatan goat leather covers the spine and corners and complements the French marbled paper.

Butterfly Stitch pamphlet book. 4½" × 6" × ½"

This leather-bound journal illustrates sewing on tapes, which are visible on the spine. Sewn headbands offer extra support at the head and tail of our thick leather journals. A medium-brown Harmatan goat leather and a Galen Berry peacock hand marble enhance this handsome book.

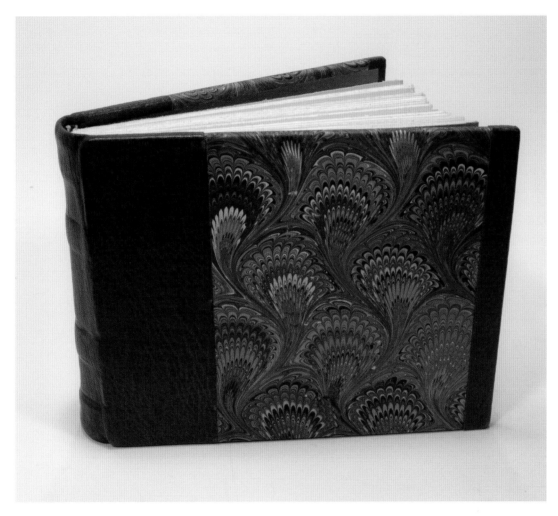

Tight-back book with hand-sewn headbands.
5½" × 6¾" × 1½"

APPENDIX

NUMERICAL WEIGHT FOR PAPER CONVERSIONS

Understanding the numerical weight of text and cover paper can be confusing. Paper weight includes various factors related to the dimensions and quantity of parent sheets, which are weighed before they are cut into various sizes. In addition, the numerical weight is expressed in two different measuring systems. One is the more well-known Imperial method, which expresses the weight in pounds (lbs.). The other and more useful method is the metric system, which expresses paper weight in grams per square meter (gsm). In addition, some papers are expressed in bond weight, which also uses pounds.

The following charts help you use the weights as a comparison tool for determining the subtle differences between, for example, a 60 lb. and 70 lb. text paper. The best method when first getting started, however, is to actually feel the paper to decide if it is appropriate for your purposes.

TEXT PAPERS

The listed text-weight papers refer to papers that are typically used for the text pages of a book. They are also the weight of most decorative papers. For reference, a 60 or 70 lb. paper would be considered in the range of a high-quality copy paper and best for two-sided printing. Most decorative papers are also in this weight category. An 80 or 90 lb. text paper might be more appropriate for a high-quality writing journal but would be on the heavier side as a decorative paper. The following are approximate conversions:

Light Text Weight
   16 lb. bond = 40 lb. text = 60 gsm
   20 lb. bond = 50 lb. text = 75 gsm

Medium Text Weight
   24 lb. bond = 60 lb. text = 90 gsm
   28 lb. bond = 70 lb. text = 105 gsm

Heavy Text Weight
   32 lb. bond = 80 lb. text = 115 gsm
   36 lb. bond = 90 lb. text = 135 gsm

COVER PAPERS

Cover-weight papers are typically used for invitations, postcards, and business cards. We would consider a 50 or 60 lb. cover-weight paper for the outside cover of a pamphlet book. A medium-weight, 70 lb. cover paper is what we use for the spine inlay of the round-back book. It could also be used as a medium-weight photo album paper. An 80 or 90 lb. cover paper can be used as a heavier-weight photo album paper. The following are approximate conversions:

Light Cover Weight
   50 lb. cover = 135 gsm
   60 lb. cover = 165 gsm

Medium Cover Weight
   70 lb. cover = 190 gsm
   80 lb. cover = 215 gsm

Heavy Cover Weight
   90 lb. cover = 250 gsm

APPROXIMATE CONVERSIONS

FRACTIONAL TO DECIMAL

¹⁄₃₂"	=	.030
¹⁄₁₆"	=	.060
³⁄₃₂"	=	.090
¹⁄₈"	=	.125
³⁄₁₆"	=	.180
¹⁄₄"	=	.250
⁵⁄₁₆"	=	.300
³⁄₈"	=	.375
⁷⁄₁₆"	=	.430
¹⁄₂"	=	.500
⁹⁄₁₆"	=	.560
⁵⁄₈"	=	.625
¹¹⁄₁₆"	=	.680
³⁄₄"	=	.750
¹³⁄₁₆"	=	.810
⁷⁄₈"	=	.875
¹⁵⁄₁₆"	=	.930
1"	=	1.00

FRACTIONAL TO METRIC (MM)

¹⁄₃₂"	=	.75
¹⁄₁₆"	=	1.5
³⁄₃₂"	=	2.5
¹⁄₈"	=	3.0
³⁄₁₆"	=	4.5
¹⁄₄"	=	6.0
⁵⁄₁₆"	=	7.5
³⁄₈"	=	9.5
⁷⁄₁₆"	=	11.0
¹⁄₂"	=	12.5
⁹⁄₁₆"	=	14.0
⁵⁄₈"	=	16.0
¹¹⁄₁₆"	=	17.5
³⁄₄"	=	19.0
¹³⁄₁₆"	=	20.5
⁷⁄₈"	=	22.0
¹⁵⁄₁₆"	=	23.5
1"	=	25.0

GLOSSARY

Further information can be found in the chapters listed at the end of each description.

adhesive: A general term used for a number of bookbinding glues. Several common adhesives are **PVA**, **PVA Thick**, wheat paste, and **methyl cellulose**. See chapters 1 and 2.

adhesive binding: A type of binding whereby only glue is used to hold the text pages together. Sometimes referred to as a perfect binding, it is used to produce a quick and inexpensively bound book. Another style of adhesive binding is a fan-glued binding.

awl: Awls are used for piercing holes into folded text pages, allowing you to insert the needle through them when sewing a text block. A thin awl that produces a hole only slightly larger than the needle and thread that pass through it is an appropriate size. See chapter 1.

backing boards: Boards used in hand binding to assist in the backing of a book. They are usually made of hard wood faced with a strip of metal. The boards are angled at the top edges for producing a shoulder along the spine. See **lying press**.

backing hammer: A traditional hammer used in rounding and backing the spine of a text block when making a round-back book. The round-back project uses a backing hammer for the rounding process only. The face of the hammer is often slightly convex and is associated with a cobbler's hammer. See chapters 1 and 6.

backing press: A large, vertically oriented press with steel plates brought together by a single screw. Used for the backing process of creating a shoulder after the book has been rounded. Also called a **job backer**. See **shoulder**. Also see chapter 1.

beeswax: A small amount of beeswax is used to prevent sewing thread from tangling. Beeswax also adds a small amount of tackiness that keeps the thread snug when sewing signatures together. See chapters 1, 4, and 5.

binder's board: See **book board**. See chapters 1 and 2.

board shear: A board shear is specifically designed for cutting book board. Most board shears will have a movable gauge for accurate cutting, a foot clamp to hold the board secure, and a heavy counterweight to prevent the blade from accidentally falling. Also known as a board cutter or board trimmer. See chapter 1.

board thickness: Book board can be obtained in various thicknesses in the range of $\frac{1}{16}$" to $\frac{1}{8}$" or greater, but it is commonly listed in thousandths of an inch. Common thicknesses range from .060 to .100. The projects in the book use .090 or $\frac{3}{32}$". See chapters 1 and 2.

bone folder: This common bookbinding tool is typically used for creasing, pressing, and scoring. Folders are usually shaped from cow bone, but Teflon folders have become increasingly popular. In bookbinding a folder is essential for defining the joint of a book. For box making it is ideal for pressing paper and book cloth into corners. See **Teflon folder**. See chapter 1.

book board: Also referred to as binder's board, book board can be obtained in various grades and thicknesses. A standard-quality and medium-density board is recommended for beginners because it is fairly easy to cut with a utility knife. A higher-quality book board, known as **Davey board**, is denser and sturdier but more difficult to cut by hand. See chapters 1 and 2.

book cloth: Book cloth is a common covering material used in bookbinding and box making. Traditional book cloth is manufactured with a starch additive that makes it nonporous and durable. Paper-backed book cloths are also available and a little easier to glue. Because of its durability, book cloth is often used for covering the hinged area along the spine of a book or box. See chapters 1 and 2.

case: Two book board pieces and a spine joined to form a cover, which is then glued as a unit to the text block in bookbinding. For box making it is the outside cover, to which the trays are attached. See chapters 4 and 5.

casing-in: The process of attaching the text block and endpapers to a case when completing a book. See chapters 4 and 5.

chapbook: Traditionally, a chapbook is a small, single- or multiple-signature pamphlet book. Today, they are thought of as a hand-bound booklet of up to fifty pages. The pamphlet book project is an example of a chapbook. See chapters 3 and 9.

clamshell box: Also referred to as a two-tray or drop-spine box. When closed, the small tray nests inside the large tray, creating a double wall that produces a solid, highly protective structure for books or other items. See chapters 7 and 9.

cover weight: A general term applied to papers slightly heavier than text weight, but not as heavy as card stock. The spine inlay used for the round-back book is an example of a cover-weight paper. See chapter 1 and the appendix.

cutting bar: A heavy straightedge used for cutting stability and safety. Cutting bars are essential when cutting book board. See chapters 1 and 2.

cutting knife: Cutting knives are needed for cutting and trimming paper, book cloth, and book board. For cutting book board, a heavy-duty knife is essential. A light-duty knife is best for cutting paper and book cloth. See chapters 1 and 2.

cutting mat: A large, self-healing cutting mat is an ideal surface for board and paper cutting. The synthetic surface allows the mat to "self-heal" after it is cut with a blade. Cutting mats, when kept clean, are also a nice surface for working on. See chapters 1 and 2.

Davey board: Often used to describe a high-quality bookbinding board. Available in varying thicknesses, it is usually single ply, dense, and warp resistant. The name Davey comes from the company that originally manufactured the board. See chapters 1 and 2.

decorative paper: Papers that have some decorative element such as color, texture, or design. Marbled and printed papers are generally used to cover books and boxes, but almost any text-weight paper could be used. See chapters 1 and 2.

drop-spine box: Name given to a clamshell box because the spine drops when the box is opened. See **clamshell box**. See chapter 7.

endpapers: A single sheet of paper that is either directly glued or folded in half, with one half glued to the inside cover and the other half, referred to as the flyleaf, kept free. See **tip-in** and **pastedown**. See chapters 4 and 5.

exposed sewing: Sewing style where the sewing is deliberately visible along the outside spine of the book. Typically seen with pamphlet books or a variety of book art structures. See chapters 3 and 9.

filler: Paper cut to the shape of the bare board on the inside covers after the turn-ins have been glued. The filler raises the height, so that when the pastedown is applied it eliminates a visible ridge.

finishing press: A small table-top press that holds a book or text bock in a vertical position, with hands-free access to the spine. It is especially useful when gluing and adding spine reinforcement, such as super, to the text block. It is also used in the "finishing" stage of making a book, such as adding decorative elements or a label to the spine. See chapter 1.

flat-back book: A traditional bookbinding style that utilizes a flat board spine and is usually less than ¾" in thickness. See chapters 4 and 9.

flexible glues: Glues that dry and remain flexible, such as **PVA** and some vegetable glues. Ideal for books and boxes that are opened and closed repeatedly. See chapters 1 and 2.

flyleaf: The flyleaf is usually a part of the endpaper. Flyleaves are the first and last sheet or sheets at the beginning and end of a book. They are either tipped-in or sewn as part of the text block. See chapters 3, 4, 5, and 9.

folder: See **bone folder** and **Teflon folder**. See chapter 1.

folio: A single folded sheet of paper resulting in two leaves and four pages. A twelve-page signature consists of three folios. See **signature**. See chapters 3, 4, and 5.

fore-edge: Front edge of a book or box. Also considered as the edge opposite the spine. See chapters 3, 4, 5, 6, and 7.

French joint: The hinge or joint formed by creating a gap, usually ⅛" to ¼", between the spine and the covers of a book or box. See chapters 4, 5, and 7.

full binding: Book that is covered completely with one material, such as book cloth or leather. See **quarter binding**.

glue gun: A glue gun can be used to quickly glue a lid to a box or tray. Using a glue gun requires accuracy because the glue dries almost instantly upon contact. A high-quality, commercial-grade model is recommended for this purpose. See chapter 1.

good side: The good side of the paper or book cloth is also the right side or the correct side. It is opposite the side you would glue on, or the same side you would want to be visible in your work. See chapter 2.

grain: The grain of book board or paper occurs during the manufacturing process. As the pulp's fibers are moved along a conveyor belt, the fibers align themselves in the direction in which the belt is moving. Book board and paper grain direction is based on the parallel orientation of these fibers. See **grain long / grain short**. See chapter 2.

grain long / grain short: When the grain is running the length or longer direction of the material, it is called grain long; when it is running the width or the shorter direction, it is called grain short. Two pieces cut the same size can be either grain long or grain short, depending on the direction of the grain when it is cut. See chapter 2.

guillotine: A machine used to cut a large stack of paper and board. It is also effective for quickly squaring these materials. Many modern guillotines are electric, but the manual models are more effective for trimming completed text blocks at the head, tail, and fore-edge. See chapter 1.

head and tail: The head refers to the top of the book from the spine to the fore-edge, and the tail refers to the bottom of the book from the spine to the fore-edge. They also correspond to the top and bottom of a box as it stands upright. See chapters 3, 4, 5, 6, and 7.

headband: Popular decorative element on most commercial books. It is also known as an endband. When they are hand-sewn into the signatures, they serve to strengthen the text block. They are located both at the head and tail of the book. See chapters 1, 4, 5, and 9.

hinge: The space or gap between the spine and the lid boards where the lid flexes upon opening and closing. See **French joint**. See chapters 4, 5, and 7.

hollow or hollow back: The space between the spine of the text block and the spine of the case. It is created by attaching a heavy, trifolded text paper, such as kraft paper, which is glued between the text block and the case. A hollow back relieves the stress on the spine and allows thicker books to open more easily. See chapter 5.

in-and-out sewing pattern: One of the most basic sewing patterns. As the name implies, the needle pulls the thread into and out of the signature. Also referred to as a running stitch. See chapters 3, 4, and 5.

inlay: Created by carefully cutting and peeling off several layers of book board to create a slightly recessed area in the board before covering and placing an image, text, or ephemera in the area that has been cut out. See **spine inlay** and **onlay**. See chapter 9.

job backer: See **backing press**.

joint: See **French joint** or **hinge**. See chapters 4 and 5.

joint rods: Narrow wire rod used to form the joint or hinge between the spine and cover boards of a book while the book is being pressed. See chapters 4 and 5.

kettle stitch: A type of stitch used to lock together signatures at the head and tail of the text block. See chapters 4 and 5.

laminate: The process of gluing together two or more pieces of paper or book board to reach a desired thickness.

landscape: Book or box with a horizontal orientation and with the spine attached along the short side of the book or tray. See **portrait**.

leaf: A single unit of a text block. Since it is two sided, a leaf always contains two pages. A folio, a sheet of paper folded in half, contains two leaves. See **flyleaf** and **folio**.

library corner: A durable book corner made without any mitered cuts. Instead, it requires making three folds; the first of which is diagonal over the corner, followed by two turn-ins that cover the diagonal fold. This is the standard corner used for library bindings.

lightweight paper: Tissue weight or papers not as heavy as text-weight papers. Generally, papers that are classified under 40 lb. / 50 gsm text.

link stitch: A type of stitch that tightens the thread between signatures and locks them together. A **kettle stitch** is a type of link stitch. See chapters 4 and 5.

lying press: A small portable press used for a variety of functions, including as a finishing press, as a backing press, and for trimming books with a special groove to accommodate a plough. See **plough**.

machine-made paper: Paper that is produced on a rapidly moving belt that forms and cuts the sheet. Many machine-made sheets of paper are prone to curling and need to be dampened prior to gluing. Most machine-made, or commercial, papers exhibit a grain direction. See chapter 2.

margin: A term used to designate the distance between two points. This includes the space between the board and the edge of the turn-in or overlap of paper or book cloth. It also includes the space between the inside lining paper and the edge of the cover boards, known as the squares. See **squares**.

"Measure twice, cut once; measure once, cut twice": Popular adage used as a reminder to ensure accuracy in measuring and ultimately cutting. See chapter 2.

methyl cellulose: A weak adhesive that is most effective when added to **PVA** to extend the drying time. It also allows PVA to spread more easily. See chapters 1 and 2.

microspatula: Long, narrow tool with one or two small spatula-shaped ends, used to apply glue in an area where it is difficult to get with a brush. It is also a valuable tool for more-delicate procedures in paper and book repair. See chapter 1.

miter: Cut made with the goal of reducing the amount of overlapping material at a corner or open edge. See **tab / tab miter** and **V-shaped miter**. See chapters 2, 4, 5, 6, and 7.

nonadhesive binding: A binding that uses no adhesives to hold it together, such as a pamphlet book and other sewn structures. See chapters 3 and 9.

onlay: Image, text, or design element adhered directly onto the surface of a book or box. See **inlay**. See chapter 9.

paper cutter: Table paper cutters have a ruler along the top edge and ½" grid marks on the table top for quick measuring and placement of paper or book cloth. A hinged blade is pulled down across the paper to be cut. See chapter 1.

paste: A variety of adhesives that are vegetable in origin. They come in a powder form and must be mixed with water to become an adhesive. More commonly used with leather and paper repair and for extending the drying time of **PVA**. See chapter 1.

pastedown: The portion of the endpaper that is glued to the inside cover of the book. See **endpapers**. See chapters 4 and 5.

plough: In hand bookbinding, a mechanical device used for trimming the edges of a text block. Although used very little since the invention of the guillotine in the 1840s, the plough remains popular among traditional fine binders.

portrait: Vertical orientation of a book or box, with the spine attached along the long side of the structure. See **landscape**.

pressing board: Pressing boards are often made of finished ¾" plywood or Plexiglas. They are used for pressing books or boxes under weights or in a book press. The board helps to distribute weight evenly over the surface of the structure. See chapter 1.

PVA: Most popular of the bookbinding adhesives, it is the abbreviation for polyvinyl acetate. This water-soluble white glue is specifically designed to maintain flexibility over a long period of time. It is also nontoxic and archival. See chapters 1 and 2.

PVA Thick: A much-thicker and much-stronger version of regular **PVA**. It works well for specific applications such as box making, or where more-viscous glue is required. See chapters 1 and 2.

quarter binding: A binding with only about one-quarter of each side of the book being covered in book cloth or leather, and the other portion in paper or another material. Similarly, there are half bindings, three-quarter bindings, and full bindings. This is primarily an aesthetic consideration, and the books in the projects fall somewhere between a quarter and half binding.

round-back book: A book that is constructed with a rounded spine. See **flat-back book** and **tight-back book**. See chapters 5 and 9.

rounding: Rounding the spine is the process of offsetting the signatures into an arc of approximately one-third of a circle, by using a hammer. This helps reduce the thickness along the spine and allows the book to open easier. See chapter 5.

sewing frame: Used for sewing signatures on tapes or cords in order to strengthen the text block. Tapes or cords are secured in a slotted base board and along a cross bar and then stretched by tightening with wooden nuts along threaded dowels. See chapter 1.

sewing-on cords: Method of sewing signatures onto cords, which come in a variety of diameters. The cords are secured to the covers to strengthen the attachment of the book to the covers. See chapter 9.

sewing-on tapes: Method of sewing signatures onto cloth tape, which typically comes in widths from ¼" to ¾". The tapes are secured to the covers to strengthen the attachment of the book to the covers. See chapters 1 and 9.

sewing thread: Sewing thread for bookbinding is typically a strong linen material that comes in varying thicknesses, from 18/3 (thicker) to 35/3 (thinner). See chapter 1.

shears: Scissors that are over 6" in length and exert more force than typical scissors.

shoulder: The right-angled groove formed in a rounded spine, into which cover boards are placed. It accommodates the thickness of the covers along the joint of a book. The process is performed on a backing press in what is traditionally called rounding and backing. See **backing boards** and **backing press**.

signature: A folded set of sheets that are ultimately sewn together to create the text block. See chapters 3, 4, and 5.

signature marks: Tick marks along the folds of signatures, indicating the sewing stations. Also used as reference marks on the signatures to ensure that the signatures are sewn in the correct order. See chapters 3, 4, and 5.

slipcase: Box structure for storage and protection of a book or books. A slipcase has one open end to allow for the easy removal of the book. See chapters 6 and 9.

Solander box: Another name for a clamshell box that incorporates a drop spine or drop front for easy removal of a book or documents.

spacing guides: Spacing guides are a great aid for making quick and repeated measurements where consistency and accuracy are important. The most common ones we use are ⅛", ¼", ³⁄₁₆", and ½". See chapter 2.

spine: The back of the book, where the signatures are folded, sewn, and reinforced. The spine also refers to the back of a box at the hinge or the back wall of a slipcase. The spine is opposite the fore-edge. See chapters 3, 4, 5, 6, and 7.

spine edge: Edge of the lid board toward the spine and opposite the fore-edge. See chapters 4, 5, 6, and 7.

spine gap: Space between the spine and boards that forms a hinge or joint. See chapters 4, 5, and 7.

spine inlay: The spine inlay serves the dual purpose of a spacing guide and a spine stiffener to help form, support, and strengthen a round-back book. The spine inlay is made of slightly stiffer or heavier paper, sometimes referred to as a cover-weight paper. See chapter 5.

spine-lining paper: The spine-lining paper is text paper applied to the spine of a book to provide a smooth surface. It is used for the attachment of a hollow tube on a rounded spine. See chapter 5.

spring divider: A tool used for making repeated quick and accurate measurements in bookbinding and box making. See chapters 1, 2, 4, 5, 6, and 7.

square: Commonly known as a Carpenter's square or an L square, used for squaring book board and paper. It also refers to a small steel machine square that we use to assist in determining the width and length of a book as well as other measurements. See chapters 1 and 2.

squares: The squares of a book refers to the even margin at the fore-edge and head and tail, where the pastedown is glued to the cover. In box making it is the even margin between the tray and the outside of the lid. Common squares are approximately ⅛" but can vary depending on the size of the book or box and aesthetic considerations. See **margin**. See chapters 4, 5, 6, and 7.

stab binding: Type of binding that requires holes to be punched or drilled through the entire book. The most popular style of stab bindings is seen in Japanese exposed sewing books.

standing press: A large, floor-model book press that can accommodate many books at the same time.

straightedge: A flat, metal ruler or cutting bar used as a guide to ensure a straight cut with a cutting knife when cutting book board, papers, and book cloth. See chapters 1 and 2.

super: Spine reinforcement material that strengthens the attachment of the text block to the covers of a book. See chapters 1, 4, and 5.

swell: The expansion of a text block along the spine, where the folds and sewing thread in the signatures add a small amount of thickness.

tab / tab miter: A small or narrow flap formed by cutting paper or book cloth. Tabs are turned in to cover a corner or open edge on a box. See chapters 2, 6, and 7.

tail: Opposite of the head of a book or box structure. See **head and tail**.

tap: Using the bone folder to tap the corners after they have been mitered and covered, which helps smooth and eliminate any burrs. It is best to perform this process soon after gluing, when the cover material is still slightly malleable. See chapters 4, 5, 6, and 7.

Teflon folder: An alternative to the standard bone folder, Teflon allows the use of more pressure on delicate papers or book cloth without burnishing or bruising the paper. See chapter 1.

text block: A collection of signatures that have been sewn together. It usually includes other components such as the tipped-in endpapers, spine reinforcement material, and headbands. See chapters 3, 4, and 5.

text weight: The weight of paper that is equal to the text pages in a book, or the weight of standard copy paper. Typical text-weight decorative papers we like to use in bookbinding and box making are marbled papers, Florentine prints, and Japanese and Indian silk-screened papers. The weight ranges from 50 lb. / 75 gsm to 100 lb. / 150 gsm. See chapters 1 and 2 and the appendix.

thick-glue applicator: Makeshift tool used to apply **PVA Thick** to the edges of book board when constructing a box. The thick-glue applicator tool is one you can easily make using a piece of book board approximately ½" wide by 3" in length. See chapters 1, 2, 6, and 7.

thick-glue scraper: Makeshift tool used to scrape off excess **PVA Thick** that oozes out along the inside walls of a box as it is being constructed. At one end, make a 45° angled cut, leaving a small straight edge of ⅛" at the tip. See chapters 2, 6, and 7.

tight-back book: A type of binding where the spine of the text block is glued directly to the spine of the case, with no spacing at the hinge. Considered a fine binding technique or style that is common with leather-bound books. See **flat-back book** and **round-back book**. See chapter 9.

tip-in: This process occurs when attaching endpapers or a single sheet of paper. It is the process of gluing a very narrow strip along the spine side of the paper to be attached to the text block. See chapters 4 and 5.

tongue tab: A very narrow tab used to cover the inside corner of a box or tray. Sometimes called a ribbon tab. See chapters 6 and 7.

tray: In box making, a three- or four-sided structure for holding objects. The tray is constructed separate from the lid. See chapter 7.

tuck-in: The process of making an inward tuck of paper or book cloth along the mitered edge after the first turn-in. The tuck-in is usually done with a bone folder or finger. It helps eliminate a slight burr from forming at the edge of the corner following the turn-in. See chapters 4, 5, 6, and 7.

turn-in: The extra ½" to ¾" length of paper or book cloth that overlaps an open edge of book board. It is folded around the board edge and glued down onto the inside surface. See chapters 4, 5, 6, and 7.

two-tray box: A name that is sometimes used to describe a **clamshell box** because it is composed of two trays. See chapter 7.

V-shaped miter: Cutting two edges of paper together at a fold to form a "V" shape, such as when mitering the outside bottom of a tray or the corner of a slipcase. This type of cut reduces more bulk than a straight cut does. See chapters 2, 6, and 7.

wall: The term used to identify the sides of a tray or box. See chapters 6 and 7.

warping: Also referred to as bowing, this occurs with book board that is not lined properly or has not dried under weights. Sometimes, warping is a product of climate conditions and cannot always be controlled. Poor-quality book board is also susceptible to warping or bowing. See chapters 2 and 6.

waste sheet: Blank newsprint, copy paper, or any other paper used as a disposable sheet. Waste sheets can be used under decorative paper or book cloth when applying glue, or as a protective sheet when placing finished work between press boards and under weights. See chapter 1.

weights: Weights are used to ensure that book board dries flat, especially after paper or book cloth has been glued to a lid or case. We have used covered bricks, heavy books, shrink-wrapped stacks of legal pads, marble slabs, soft weights, and many other heavy objects. See chapters 1 and 2.

BOOK AND BOX MAKING RESOURCES

BOOKS

The following books are recommended for traditional bookbinding and box making.

Bannister, Manly. *The Craft of Bookbinding*. New York: Dover, 1975.

Brown, Margaret R., and Don Etherington. *Boxes for the Protection of Rare Books: Their Design and Construction*. Washington, DC: Library of Congress, 1982.

Hollander, Annette. *Bookcraft*. New York: Van Nostrand Reinhold, 1974.

Hollander, Tom, and Cindy Hollander. *Constructing and Covering Boxes*. Atglen, PA: Schiffer, 2009.

Johnson, Arthur. *The Thames and Hudson Manual of Bookbinding*. London: Thames and Hudson, 1978.

Johnson, Pauline. *Creative Bookbinding*. New York: Dover, 1963.

Lewis, A. B. *Basic Bookbinding*. New York: Dover, 1952.

Lindsay, Jen. *Fine Binding: A Technical Guide*. New Castle, DE: Oak Knoll, 2009.

Roberts, Matt T., and Don Etherington. *Bookbinding and the Construction of Books: A Dictionary of Descriptive Terminology*. Washington, DC: Library of Congress, 1982.

Smith, Keith A. *Non-adhesive Binding*. Rochester, NY: Keith Smith Books, 1990.

Watson, Aldren. *Hand Bookbinding*. New York: Dover, 1986.

Young, Laura S. *Bookbinding and Conservation by Hand: A Working Guide*. New York: R. B. Bowker, 1981.

SCHOOLS AND ORGANIZATIONS

Bookbinding and box making workshops are offered at a number of schools and book art centers, including those listed below.

American Academy of Bookbinding
PO Box 1590, 300 South Townsend Avenue, Telluride, CO 81435
Phone: 970-728-3886
Website: www.ahhaa.org

Canadian Bookbinders & Book Artists Guild (CBBAG)
60 Atlantic Avenue, Suite 112, Toronto, ON, Canada M6K 1X9
Phone: 416-581-1071
Website: www.cbbag.ca

Center for Book Arts
28 West 27th Street, 3rd Floor, New York, NY 10001
Phone: 212-481-0295
Website: centerforbookarts.org

Garage Annex School for Book Arts
One Cottage Street #5, Room 503, Easthampton, MA 01027
Phone: 413 527-8044
Website: www.garageannexschool.com

Guild of Book Workers
521 Fifth Avenue, New York, NY 10175-0083
Website: guildofbookworkers.org
The Guild of Book Workers is a great organization for resources, events, and study opportunities.

Hollander's Book & Paper Arts Workshops
410 North Fourth Avenue, Ann Arbor, MI 48104
Phone: 734-741-7531
Website: www.hollanders.com

Minnesota Center for Book Arts (MCBA)
1011 S Washington Avenue #100, Minneapolis, MN 55415
Phone: 612-215-2520
Website: www.mnbookarts.org

Morgan Conservatory
1754 East 47th Street, Cleveland, OH 44103
Phone: 216-361-9255
Website: www.morganconservatory.org

North Bennet Street School
150 North Street, Boston, MA 02109
Phone: 617-227-0155
Website: www.nbss.edu

San Francisco Center for the Book
300 DeHaro Street, San Francisco, CA 94103
Phone: 415-565-0545
Website: sfcb.org

SUPPLIERS

Art and craft supply stores carry some of the basic tools needed for bookbinding and box making, such as scissors, brushes, cutting mats, and knives. However, some supplies such as book board and book cloth and a few specialized hand tools can be difficult to find. These are some of the more reliable suppliers that we know of. Searching the internet by using "bookbinding tools" or "bookbinding supplies" as key words may be helpful.

Bindery Tools, LLC
190 Martin Road, Myerstown, PA 17067
Phone: 717-866-2506
Website: www.binderytools.com
Source for mostly used bookbinding equipment such as book presses and board shears

Hollander's
410 North Fourth Ave, Ann Arbor, MI 48104
Phone: 734-741-7531
Website: www.hollanders.com
Source for bookbinding tools and supplies, decorative papers, board-cutting services, bookbinding and box making kits

John Neal, Bookseller
1833 Spring Garden Street, Greensboro, NC 27403
Phone: 336-272-6139
Website: www.johnnealbooks.com
Source for bookbinding tools and supplies

TALAS
330 Morgan Avenue, Brooklyn, NY 11211
Phone: 212-219-0770
Website: www.talasonline.com
Source for bookbinding tools and supplies

1. Plan your work in advance. When using this book, it is most effective to first read through all of the steps in each part before proceeding.

2. Keep all of your tools and materials organized. It is also helpful to lightly label the papers and book cloth on the back for quick and easy identification.

3. When sewing signatures, make sure the thread is pulled taut and parallel to the spine to avoid sewing with slack in the thread.

4. Brush outward from the center of your materials when gluing. Glue on a waste sheet such as newsprint or old copy paper, and remember to hold the paper or book cloth down firmly to prevent shifting and getting glue on the "good" side of your materials.

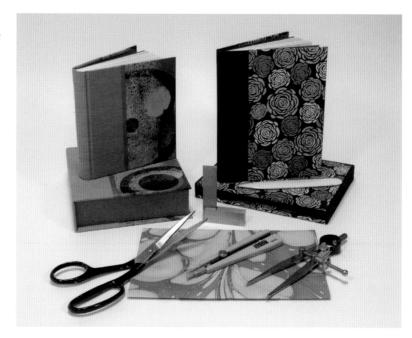

5. Certain machine-made papers may curl as soon as you apply glue to them. To prevent this, slightly dampen the paper with a sponge to allow it to first curl and then "relax."

6. When using PVA glue, if it seems a little thick, add a very small amount of water to thin it slightly. DO NOT dilute the Thick PVA glue, however, as it will clump.

7. Re-apply glue to areas that might have dried during the gluing process. At the same time, be careful to not over-glue these areas in order to prevent glue from unexpectedly oozing.

8. An X-Acto knife or microspatula can be used as a tool for touching up small unglued or dry areas. Place a small amount of glue on the blade and carefully slide it under the unglued area.

9. Work with a good quality pair of scissors. We recommend one with a sharp point that will cut through glued paper and book cloth easily. Keep your scissors clean to help keep your cuts crisp.

10. A spring divider, as described in the book, is a handy tool for quick and concise measuring.

11. Most corners should be mitered at a 45 degree angle and at $1\frac{1}{2}$ to 2 times the thickness of the board. If your cuts are much more than this, the corners will appear bulky. If they are much less, the board may not be completely covered.

12. A bone folder is one of the most common tools used by bookbinders. It is used for scoring and creasing paper, pressing down paper and cloth, helping to remove air pockets and wrinkles, rounding corners, pressing down edges, and getting into tight spots.

13. Grain direction of book board, paper, and book cloth is a significant consideration in bookbinding and box making. Lightly bending your materials will help in determining the grain direction of all your materials as being either long or short.

14. The use of weights, such as heavy books or covered bricks, are important for allowing your finished products to lay flat after drying. It is best to allow weights to remain in place overnight or longer.

15. Good quality tools and materials will help you get the most out of your bookbinding and box making experiences.

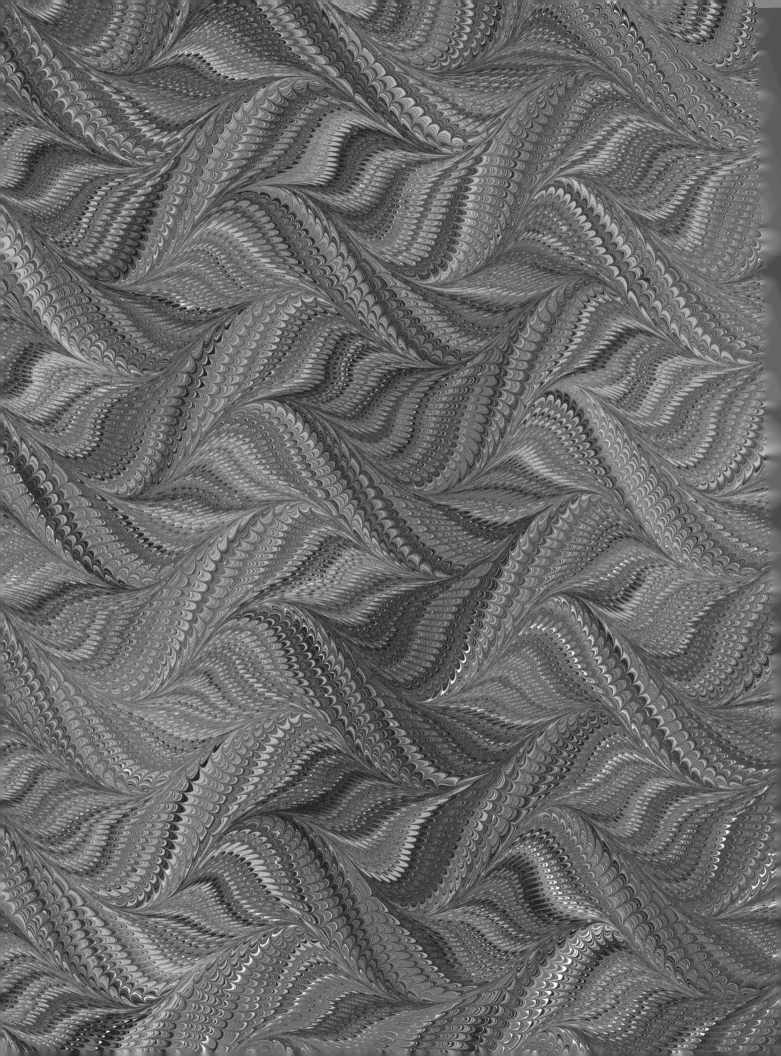